A Guide to Policies for Energy Conservation

A Guide to Policies for Energy Conservation

The European Experience

Edited by

Frank J. Convery

Heritage Trust Professor of Environmental Studies,
and Director of the Environmental Institute at University
College Dublin, Ireland

Edward Elgar

Cheltenham, UK • Northampton, MA, USA

Published by
Edward Elgar Publishing Limited
Glensanda House
Montpellier Parade
Cheltenham
Glos GL50 1UA
UK

Edward Elgar Publishing Company
6 Market Street
Northampton
Massachusetts 01060
USA

A catalogue record for this book is available from the British Library

Library of Congress Cataloguing in Publication Data
A guide to policies for energy conservation: the European experience
  /edited by Frank J. Convery.
    Includes index.
      1. Energy policy—Europe. 2. Energy conservation—Europe.
    I. Convery, Frank J.
    HD9502.E82G84   1998
    333.79'16'094—dc21   98–6256
                                                                  CIP

ISBN 1 85898 635 4

Contents

Figures

Tables

Contributors

Kornelis Blok, Department of Science, Technology and Society, Utrecht University

A. Bonduelle, INESTENE, Paris

Michel Colombier, ICE, Paris

Frank J. Convery, Environmental Institute, University College Dublin

Edelgard Gruber, Fraunhofer Institute for Systems and Innovation Research (ISI), Karlsruhe, Germany

Chris Hendriks, Department of Science, Technology and Society, Utrecht University

John Lawlor, Economic and Social Research Institute, Dublin

Craig Mickle, Association for the Conservation of Energy, London

P. Radanne, INESTENE, Paris

Kenya Tillerson, ICE, Paris

Jan Willem Velthuijsen, Stichting voor Economisch Onderzoek (SEO), University of Amsterdam

Ernst Worrell, Department of Science, Technology and Society, Utrecht University

Introduction

Frank J. Convery

OBJECTIVES

Firms, households, public enterprises all have numerous opportunities to conserve energy which they do not act upon. Why is this? They may be ill-informed, policy may discourage them from taking positive action, the value of the savings achieved may not justify the costs of doing so.

A range of policy initiatives have been taken in a number of European countries in an effort to tackle these constraints. How effective have they been? What can we learn from our endeavours in this regard?

It was decided to undertake an *ex post* analysis of the performance of a range of policy instruments which have been utilized to encourage energy conservation, with a view to assessing the benefits and costs yielded thereby and identifying the lessons for instrument design. The following instruments were analysed: government investment and subsidies – experience in Ireland, Denmark, Germany and the UK; information and education – consultation analysed in Germany; regulation and other instruments – the case of combined heat and power in the European Union; demand-side management in the UK and other countries; institutional design – regional implementation of energy conservation in France. For each of these, an effort was made to assess whether the policy instrument in question as used:

- yielded private (financial) benefits in terms of energy conservation and related benefits, which exceeded their costs;
- generated other benefits and costs (an attempt was also made to quantify the magnitude of the external costs and benefits);
- generated insights and guidelines for those in the policy process as to the strengths and weaknesses of various instruments in different situations, and the lessons that could be provided for the design and implementation of policy in the future.

CONTEXT

In the context of identifying opportunities for achieving reductions in carbon dioxide (CO_2) emissions, the Directorate-General for Science, Research and Technology (DGXII of the Commission of the European Communities (CEC)) commissioned a research project designed to identify and cost the opportunities for energy conservation. The findings were reported in CEC (1991, 1994a). The main conclusion was that there was a very large potential to achieve energy conservation and thereby reduce emissions, and that some of these opportunities should already be financially viable, in the sense that the financial benefits of reduced energy consumption should be sufficient to justify investment in conservation. It was a prospective study, looking forward. A parallel research project was initiated by the Commission to identify and estimate the external costs – those costs not borne by perpetrator – associated with electric power generation (Externe project). These include health costs, damage to crops and building fabric and so on as a result of power generation (on a life-cycle analysis basis) which are not borne directly by the power producers (CEC, 1994a).

In the context of these two large research projects, the team which comprises the contributors to this volume addressed two questions: If there are indeed good 'commercial' opportunities for energy conservation, why are they not already being taken up? Second, what lessons can be learnt from existing policy initiatives which have been implemented with the objective of achieving energy conservation? This book addresses the second question.

In regard to the first question – why are consumers and producers not investing in energy conservation? – the findings are presented in detail in Convery (1994) and summarized below.

Divergence in Assumptions

The main sources of such divergence are the following: in the CEC (1991, 1994b) study:

- the 'conventional wisdom' on future oil and coal prices is assumed, namely an oil price of $30 (1987) per barrel and a coal price of $60 per tonne in 2010. It is unlikely that those faced with making conservation investments are applying such high energy prices in their (implicit or explicit) calculations;
- a discount rate in the range of 5–8 per cent per year was used. For many potential investors in energy conservation, the rate they would apply is much higher than this.

The combined effect of these two assumptions would be a substantial overestimate of the volume of conservation investment which would be judged to be 'commercial' by the private sector.

The 'Wedge' Role of Transaction Costs

The fixed costs involved (mainly in terms of scarce management time) in learning about opportunities, filling out forms, the cost sharing of small grants and administering them, can all be regarded as transactions costs or barriers to entry, which must be surmounted in order to learn about, evaluate, implement and operate an energy conservation opportunity. The magnitude of such costs can simply overwhelm any likely payoff of such an effort, such that they act as a performance-inhibiting 'wedge' which prevents action being undertaken which could be commercially and/or economically viable.

Such transaction costs are typically not costed, but they are the key factors which explain why seemingly viable conservation opportunities are not undertaken. There are policy initiatives which can be taken to reduce the inhibitory effects of such transactions costs, but these must be carefully designed and meet certain criteria if they are to be effective. The transaction cost problem is especially severe in the case of small and medium-sized enterprises (SMEs) and households.

Here are two examples of evidence as to why transactions costs are so central:

1. We found that householders in Ireland have a range of conservation opportunities which are financially viable but are not undertaken: they lack knowledge of the opportunities; the aggregate returns in absolute terms are large, but per householder are small, so that the costs of finding out about the opportunities, what to do about them, and then acting on them, are such that, individually, they do not avail themselves of the opportunities.
2. The same considerations apply in the case of small and medium-sized industry in Germany where general ignorance of opportunities is also important. The mechanisms put in place to address this deficiency demonstrably fail to do so and indeed may compound the problem.

Inadequate Information

For industry in general in the Netherlands, concerns about reliability and implications for quality predominate as explanations by industry managers as to why they do not undertake seemingly commercially viable conservation investment.

Perverse Incentives

There are demand-side management (DSM) related conservation investment opportunities available to electricity consumers in the UK which would cost less to implement than the value of the fuel saved, but they do not take advantage of them for two reasons: the pricing structure they face and the incentives faced by the utilities do not encourage such action, and there are barriers in terms of lack of information (and time) on the part of consumers which inhibit action. The second category of inhibition can be classified as a transaction cost.

If public policy could achieve economies of scale such that the average cost of transactions are very substantially reduced, then some conservation activities which were previously unviable would become commercially feasible.

A number of action pointers for those in the policy process who wish to encourage effective energy conservation emerged. In terms of what can be done today to improve performance these actions include:

- identifying the 'real' commercial conservation potential (the commercially achievable reality is much lower than the estimates);
- reducing the costs of transacting the business of conservation to a minimum (small grants and large amounts of paperwork are a waste of time);
- not wasting time with DSM unless it is intended to make it pay for utilities;
- perceiving energy is an 'essential good' which poor people cannot do without; when using price- and tax-related measures to achieve conservation, ensuring that those least able to absorb the (higher) prices are compensated;
- making subsidiarity more than a slogan by having the EU and national governments set an appropriate policy framework and acting as *animateurs* for energy conservation, but vesting responsibility for action on the ground in industry associations, tenant groups, or in general as close to the grass roots as possible (general data and exhortation are a waste of time; the information and the programme must relate precisely to the needs and knowledge of those 'at the coal face');
- not initiating conservation policies unless there is the capacity and willingness to evaluate performance and to act on the results (without them, dysfunctional policies can – and do – go on for ever).

THIS BOOK

It is this last point – looking critically at past performance – which stimulated the research reported on in this book.

There is an increasing – but still relatively small – volume of analytical literature which attempts to evaluate the performance of policies which have been initiated to address environmental and energy conservation performance. The work of Hanley (1993), Hahn (1989), Bergman *et al.* (1993) and Tietenberg (1994) are typical of efforts to analyse policy *ex post* with a view to improving design and performance.

Hahn (1989, p. 21) notes that both normative and positive theorizing could greatly benefit from a careful examination of the results of recent innovative approaches to environmental management. It is in this spirit that this book has been written.

ACKNOWLEDGEMENTS

The research on which this book is based was supported financially by the European Commission (Directorate General XII) under the JOULE 2 programme. We are very grateful to Pierre Valette and numerous other Commission officials who took the time and trouble to provide encouragement, advice and feedback at critical times. They bear no responsibility for errors or omissions.

REFERENCES

Bergman, Hans, Ola Jörnstedt, and Kerstin Lófgren (1993), *Five Economic Instruments in Swedish Environmental Policy*, Stockholm: Swedish Environmental Protection Agency.

Commission of the European Communities (CEC) (1991), *Cost-effectiveness Analysis of CO_2 Reduction Options (CO_2 Study – 'CRASH' Programme)*, Brussels: Directorate General for Science, Research and Technology.

Commission of the European Communities (CEC) (1994a), *Achievements and Results of the ExternE Project*, Brussels: CEC.

Commission of the European Communities (CEC) (1994b), *Cost-effectiveness Analysis of Energy Technologies and CO_2 Abatement Strategies: Up-date of the CRASH Programme: The case of Five EC Countries: Germany, France, Italy, the Netherlands, United Kingdom*, prepared by COHERENCE, Belgium, Brussels: Directorate General for Science, Research and Technology.

Convery, Frank J. (ed.) (1994), *Energy Conservation–Opportunities Not Taken*, Environmental Institute, Ireland: University College Dublin (mimeo).

Hahn, Robert W. (1989), *A Primer on Environmental Policy Design*, London and New York: Harwood.

Hanley, Nick (1993), 'Controlling water pollution using market mechanisms: results from empirical studies', in R. Kerry Turner (ed.), *Sustainable Environmental Economics and Management: Principles and Practice*, London and New York: Belhaven Press, pp. 360–82.

Tietenberg, T.H.G. (1994), *Economics and Environmental Policy*, Aldershot, UK and Vermont, USA: Edward Elgar.

1. Government investment and subsidies: experience in Ireland, the United Kingdom, the Netherlands, Germany and Denmark

John Lawlor

This chapter examines from a cost-benefit viewpoint a number of energy conservation schemes financed by governments in various European countries. Quantitative data are used where available; however, in many cases these were not available or were incomplete. Qualitative data, where informative, have also been used. External costs and benefits are stated in physical quantities but are not valued in the body of the chapter. There is an attempt to value these external costs in Appendix III, but as explained in the appendix the results are not very satisfactory. Conclusions are drawn which distil the policy lessons from each country's experience, and recommendations are made on this basis. Unless otherwise stated, all prices are stated in 1994 ECUs.

IRELAND

Despite numerous policy statements (McSharry, 1993), there has been little government action in the area of energy conservation in Ireland in the last two decades or so. This is reflected in the government's annual energy conservation budget, which up till 1994 has been very small: it is necessary to go back to the early 1980s to find a 'real' government subsidy or investment scheme in this area. During 1994 the budget was increased by several orders of magnitude; this will see expenditure increase significantly, including that on many areas dealt with in this chapter.

Programmes we examine here include pilot projects in public sector office buildings and hospitals, which have shown the benefits of investments. However, the government has not then provided the capital to extend this to the wider public sector building stock. Because public sector bodies generally cannot borrow, if local managers want to implement energy conservation in their buildings they have had to do so within their own budgets. Until recently these have been estimated on an annual basis, therefore in general only those projects with a payback of less than one year have been undertaken.[1] This has excluded many of the energy-saving opportunities available. A further disincentive is that the savings made by such investments have tended to be absorbed by the central government via a budget reduction. Therefore there was no benefit to a public body, or part thereof, if it achieved savings on its energy bill; in fact, there has been a cost in so far as energy conservation uses up scarce management and staff time. Recent changes to public sector budgeting procedures, whereby budgets are set for three-year periods, may improve this situation.

The only other relevant project that we could find is a small-scale one which subsidizes a private organization to train long-term unemployed people to insulate the homes of low-income households.

Each of these areas is now dealt with in detail.

Government Subsidies to the Household Sector

Attic insulation grant scheme (1980–82)
The grant covered one-third of the costs of insulating attics, subject to a maximum of ECU120. Total grants paid out amounted to ECU3 million. The take-up rate represented approximately 3 per cent (29 000) of the households in the state. Table 1.1 shows that the scheme was successful in terms of costs and benefits.

However, the grant scheme was open to all households, regardless of income, and therefore it is probable that some proportion of the grant fund was taken up by middle- or higher-income groups (research into a similar scheme in the mid-1980s showed that uptake was spread very evenly between income groupings). The grant schemes should be focused at low-income groups, since high-income groups should be able to take commercially viable conservation measures without the aid of a grant.[2] In addition, the results in the table assume that there were no 'free riders'.[3] In reality there would probably be some, and therefore the results in the table are to some degree overstated; however, it is not possible to quantify this.

It is important to encourage energy efficiency among low-income households because they have usually implemented fewer conservation measures, therefore greater potential savings exist. However, research from the UK indicates that lower-income households also tend to take a high proportion of the savings in the form of more heat, thus reducing the effectiveness of schemes from a pure energy efficiency point of view. We will return to this point later.

Table 1.1   Attic insulation grant scheme, 1980–82

Total costs (000s 1994 ECU)	9,497
Private benefits (annual): energy saved[a] (000s 1994 ECU)	2,677
Private benefits vs total costs[b]	
Net present value[c] (000s 1994 ECU)	23,870
Internal rate of return (%)	28
Simple payback (years)	3.5
Energy saving (annual) (TOE)[e]	10,600
Public benefits: Reductions in emissions (tonnes per annum):	
carbon dioxide (CO_2)	50,154
sulphur dioxide (SO_2)	326
nitrogen oxides (NO_x)	91
volatile organic compounds (VOC)	65
carbon monoxide (CO)	504
Employment effects from installation Work years generated	200
and manufacture[d] Per million ECU expended	20

Notes:
[a] Energy savings are calculated on the basis that no element of savings was used to purchase more energy, and that there were no 'free riders' among recipients.
[b] In this and subsequent tables, the rate of discount used for calculating net present value is 5 per cent. The lifespan of the installations is taken to be 20 years. Strictly speaking, net present value is the best measure to use. Simple payback is not appropriate, especially for public programmes; however it is included here because it is widely used and understood.
[c] The use of different inflation indices for costs and for energy saved to update these items has a significant effect on the benefits vs costs calculation. For example, if the consumer price index had been used for both costs and fuel saved, the net present value would have been in excess of ECU40 million. This demonstrates the effect of falling real fuel prices on the economic viability of energy conservation measures.
[d] Employment effects are calculated from the labour content of a typical attic insulation contract, and from the employment and turnover statistics on Irish insulation manufacturers.
[e] TOE = tonnes of oil equivalent

Source: McSharry 1993; Lowndes (1994).

'Energy action' programme
This is a small-scale publicly funded programme to insulate the houses of low-income and elderly people, and to provide energy conservation education, while training unemployed people to UK City and Guilds certification levels. Government subvention is on two levels: it funds the training programme and also makes a small direct grant to the project. The scheme is based on a similar initiative in Scotland. It should be noted that energy conservation is only part of the aim of this project. Improving the well-being of low-income households, both in terms of increased comfort and better health, and providing marketable skills to the long-term unemployed are the main aims. Indeed, evidence from

the UK on similar schemes indicates that 60 to 80 per cent of savings are spent on increased heat levels, implying that only modest energy savings *per se* are achieved by such schemes. Anecdotal evidence from Energy Action indicates that a similar situation would apply in Ireland. This is not built into the calculations on money savings in Table 1.2; however, it is taken into account for the calculations of energy savings and emission reductions. The table gives an analysis of the scheme for one year of operation: 1993–4.[4] It shows that the scheme is effective in terms of costs and benefits.

Table 1.2   *Energy Action programme, 1993–4, with shadow price of long-term unemployed = 0*

Total costs (incl. net training grant) (000s 1994 ECU)	293
Private benefits (annual) (000s 1994 ECU)	118
Private benefits vs total costs	
Net present value (000s 1994 ECU)	768
Internal rate of return (%)	39
Simple payback (years)	2.5
Energy saving (annual) (TOE)	83
Public benefits: reductions in emissions (annual) (tonnes)	
CO_2	344
Others	negligible
Employment effects	positive
Health benefits	positive

Notes:
1. Money savings are calculated by reference to the cost of producing the same amount of warmth before and after the installation. Energy and emissions savings are calculated on the basis that 70 per cent of potential money savings are spent on purchasing more heat. This explains the low emission reductions recorded.
2. Assumed length of life of the installations varies between 10 and 20 years.

Source: Energy Action Ltd, McGettigan (1993), Condon (1994), Scott (1992), McSharry (1993).

One assumption was that the opportunity cost (that is, the shadow price) of long-term unemployed people taking part in this programme was nil. Given the level of long-term unemployment in Ireland, this appears reasonable. The implication is that the costs of labour (their training grant) in the table are net of the unemployment benefits that the trainees would have received anyway had they not been on the programme. This approach is open to argument. If the view had been taken that the shadow price of the trainees' labour was equal to their unemployment benefits (that is, labour is valued at their full grant), then the picture would have been somewhat different, as Table 1.3 shows. The programme is still worthwhile, in terms of costs and benefits, but obviously is not as favourable as portrayed in Table 1.2.

Table 1.3   Energy Action programme, 1993–4, with shadow price of long-term unemployed = unemployment benefits

Total costs (incl total training grant) (000s 1994 ECU)	384
Private benefits (annual) (000s 1994 ECU)	118
Private benefits vs total costs	
Net present value (000s 1994 ECU)	677
Internal rate of return (%)	29
Simple payback (years)	3.3
Public benefits and energy savings	as in Table 1.2

Source: Energy Action Ltd, McGettigan (1993), Condon (1994), Scott (1992), McSharry (1993).

Employment benefits   Energy Action has a small number of permanent staff. Apart from them, the energy conservation work is carried out by trainees, who are employed on the scheme for one year. The yearly intake of trainees is approximately 25. The potential employment benefits come from former trainees of the scheme increasing the supply of trained labour on the market or establishing energy conservation firms. There are no follow-up data on the employment results of former trainees, but a small number are known to have joined or set up such businesses. Indirect employment effects would flow from the manufacture of materials used on the training scheme, but this would be negligible as materials form a small proportion of the overall cost of the scheme.

Health benefits   There are probably positive health effects to be achieved from such programmes, although these have not been quantified. However, UK research indicates total extra health costs due to adverse housing conditions of ECU380 per inhabitant per year (Hunt and Boardman, 1994). The housing problems cited are similar to those found in Ireland, therefore it might be expected that the health cost per inhabitant would be of the same order of magnitude. The Energy Action scheme dealt with approximately 1200 households in the year under review. Average occupancy per household in Ireland is 3.53 (Government of Ireland, 1991); given that many of the beneficiaries of the scheme are older people and flat-dwellers, who generally live in smaller households, an occupancy rate among beneficiaries of (say) two may be assumed. This suggests possible health costs due to inadequate housing of over ECU0.9 million for the households in question. How much of this might be saved due to the project is open to conjecture.

Government Investment in Public Sector Buildings

Office buildings

This pilot project in the Department of Transport, Energy and Communications (DTEC) was never developed further. It was carried out during 1990 and 1991 and consisted of an energy audit and the implementation of the audit's recommendations. It involved four buildings, but cost-benefit analyses appear to have been carried out on only two of these. The work done consisted of the replacement of light fittings, the installation of lighting controls and the conversion from oil to natural gas central heating. As Table 1.4 shows, the programme was worthwhile for the two buildings in question.

Table 1.4   Department of Transport, Energy and Communication (DTEC) pilot project on office buildings, 1990 and 1991

Total costs (000s 1994 ECU)	71
Private benefits (annual) (000s 1994 ECU)	20
Private benefits vs total costs	
Net present value (000s 1994 ECU)	103
Internal rate of return (%)	28
Simple payback (years)	3.48
Energy saving (annual) (TOE)	35
Public benefits: reductions in emissions (annual) (tonnes)	
CO_2	360
Others	negligible
Employment effects	positive

Note: Assumed length of life of the installations varies between 10 and 20 years.

Source: Brabazon (1992), McGettigan (1993), Condon (1994), Scott (1992), McSharry (1993).

The buildings had a combined area of 13 000M², and energy usage was between 1.5 and 1.6 Gj/m² per annum before the above project was implemented.[5] The project effected savings of 23 per cent on the buildings' energy costs.

These figures are impressive in that both buildings were built in the 1980s and were considered quite energy-efficient at the time. It suggests that greater savings might be achieved in older buildings. As a rough indication of the potential savings, the total government estate of office buildings is 390 000 m² (Office of Public Works, 1993). Extrapolating by reference to the above buildings gives a potential saving across the entire government estate of perhaps ECU3 million in terms of net present value. However, a full energy audit of the government estate would be needed to obtain a more accurate figure.

Employment effects of this project are positive, in terms of manufacture and installation of new equipment, but they are very small. Larger employment effects would flow from a wider programme covering the government estate, but without knowing the nature of work required it is not possible to quantify this. As a footnote, the DTEC is at present undertaking an energy audit of all its buildings and is planning to implement the recommendations of the audit.

Hospitals

The Irish Department of Health's energy bill in 1989 was ECU35.6 million, or approximately 1.8 per cent of its total costs. This percentage had fallen from 2.6 per cent in 1984, due to falling fuel prices and energy conservation measures. A survey of 1989 energy costs in 60 per cent of Irish hospitals with a total energy bill of ECU16 million estimated that further potential savings of 20 per cent were possible (O'Malley, 1990). This represents a potential saving of ECU3.2 million per annum in the hospitals in question, and could be achieved by bringing the energy performance of all hospitals up to a 'satisfactory' level. Average energy usage at present in Irish hospitals is 1.75 Gj/m^2 (Condon, 1994).

Table 1.5   Energy conservation in hospitals in Ireland

	Pilot Project (A)	Western H.B. (2 hospitals) (B)	South-east H.B. (C)
Year of completion	1990	1993	1989
Total costs (000s 1994 ECU)	658	165	52
Private benefits (annual) (000s 1994 ECU)			
Energy	234	210	47
Non-energy	122	77	15
Total	356	287	62
Private benefits vs total costs			
Net present value (000s 1994 ECU)	3,780	3,330	718
Internal rate of return (%)	54.1	145	118
Simple payback (years)	1.8	0.8	0.8
Energy saving (annual) (TOE)	815	393	132
Public benefits: Reductions in emissions (annual) (tonnes)			
CO_2	3,900	1,500	1,400
CO	100	130	35
Others	negligible	negligible	negligible
Employment effects	negative	negative	negative

Sources: McGettigan (1993), Condon (1994), Scott (1992), McSharry (1993).

The hospital situation is similar to that of office buildings, in that a successful pilot project was instigated which, at the time of writing (1996), has not been followed up by a more broadly based programme. Table 1.5, column (A), shows the details. This hospital was converted from turf and oil to natural gas, and also from a centralized heating system to a decentralized one. Savings of 70 per cent of energy costs were achieved (Condon, 1994). This would seem to give credence to the potential savings figures quoted above – if anything, it suggests that potential savings are even greater. Considerable reductions in emissions are possible as a result of conversion to cleaner fuels such as natural gas. However, the move to more modern heating systems and to less bulky fuels has meant a fall in direct employment, as the reduction in non-energy costs indicates.

While central government has not provided funds to enable a more widespread programme to be implemented, much has been done by regional health boards and hospital engineers. As in the case of the pilot project, this work has mainly related to the decentralization of heating schemes and a change to cleaner and more efficient fuels (usually from coal, peat and fuel oil to natural gas or gas oil). It has, however, been subject to severe institutional constraints:

1. The inability to borrow, which has meant that investments have had to be made out of annual energy and maintenance budgets; as a result, only those projects with very short paybacks have been undertaken. The corollary of this has been that many, if not most, energy-saving projects have had to be forgone because they did not meet this payback criterion. These constraints are reflected in the following quotation from one internal regional health board document:

    > The payback period is the only yardstick to measure the viability of projects. The payback in most cases is less than two years. Funding can sometimes be a problem in that we have to rely on the severely cut maintenance budget to finance these projects. This problem has been overcome to a great extent by financing short payback projects from the energy budget. (Deering, 1989)

    One way around this has been to implement projects in annual phases over a number of years. This has been possible in the case of the decentralization of heating systems, but of course savings are forgone by not implementing projects more quickly;
2. Annual budget procedures: in the past, savings made have tended to be absorbed by central government, thus reducing the incentive for managers to undertake cost-saving projects. This has meant that energy-saving projects have been 'left to the initiative of the enthusiastic', in the words of one Department of Health official.

Recent changes in budgetary procedures, as described earlier (p. 7), may improve this situation.

We have some information from regional health boards which shows impressive results, but this reflects the fact that only projects with very short payback periods would be undertaken in the first place. Details are in Table 1.5, columns (B) and (C).

The data in column (B) are from two hospitals in an ongoing programme of eight hospitals, undertaken in 1993 and 1994. The programme for all eight hospitals, involving boiler system and fuel conversion, had an estimated capital cost of ECU510 000, and estimated annual savings of ECU700 000 in energy costs and ECU250 000 in non-energy costs.

The data in column (C) refer to part of a programme of energy conservation in the health board in question which appointed an energy manager in 1985. The project, relating to boiler and fuel conversion, was one of a number put in place. Overall, the board's annual energy bill was reduced by a total of ECU860 000 between 1985 and 1989, after correcting for fuel price reductions and temperature differences (Deering, 1989). This represented a reduction of 23 per cent over the period, and was achieved by better monitoring of fuel usage, the installation of energy management systems, and capital investment in new heating systems.

To summarize, a considerable amount of work has been carried out to make Irish hospitals more energy efficient. However, most of this has been done on the ground, on the initiative of individual energy managers and regional health boards. Central government has not provided any meaningful funding for the work. This has meant that only those projects with a very short payback period have been undertaken. A study in 1989 found that further savings of perhaps 20 per cent were achievable by bringing the performance of all hospitals up to the level of the better performers. However, these savings will be difficult to achieve under current restrictive budgeting procedures. As O'Malley (1989) concludes: 'further energy savings require larger capital investment with longer payback periods'. The increase in government expenditure on energy conservation in the coming years may provide more funds for this area.

Conclusion

Public investment and subsidies for energy efficiency measures in Ireland up to 1994 have been modest, despite the proven potential for substantial savings. But there is now a considerably expanded programme – with EU financial support – with funding provided to 1999. The emphasis is on provision of information and grant aid to industry (Irish Energy Centre, 1997).

UNITED KINGDOM

The UK government operates energy conservation grant schemes for both the household and the business sectors, although it has been more active in the former and more information is available for this sector.

Government Subsidies to the Household Sector

The UK has been operating a grant scheme for draught-proofing and loft insulation of houses since 1978; in 1988 the scheme was restricted to low-income houses: 'prior to this date, most grants were going to better-off families' (Boardman, 1991b). In 1990 the scheme was replaced by the Home Energy Efficiency Scheme (HEES). This and another scheme for public housing are dealt with in the following sub-sections (which quote extensively from National Audit Office, 1994).

The Home Energy Efficiency Scheme (HEES)
This scheme, started in 1990, provides grants towards basic insulation of up to ECU400 to low-income households (as defined by receipt of various state benefits). Out of a total eligible population of 6.4 million households, over 600,000 had participated in the scheme by the end of 1993. The total budget for 1994–5 was ECU96 million to cover 400,000 households (an increase from ECU48 million in 1993–4, ECU46 million in 1992–3 and ECU32 million in 1991–2). This expansion is designed to attract a wider range of beneficiaries; for example, from 1 April 1994 pensioners are eligible for the first time. The scheme is administered by a private non-profit company, Energy Action Grant Agency (EAGA), which is paid a management fee related to the value of grant payments, approximately ECU5.1 million per annum.

The scheme currently pays 100 per cent of the costs of draught-proofing, loft insulation and energy advice, up to a total of ECU400 per recipient (prior to 1994 the recipient paid a small contribution of ECU10–20). The work can be done by approved contractors[6] or by the householders themselves.

An interim evaluation of the scheme found that potential savings per household were ECU50 per annum, compared with an installation cost per household of ECU180. This indicated a simple payback of 3.5 years,[7] but was based on the premise that dwellings were heated to 'full comfort conditions' before and after installation (EAGA, 1994). Actual energy bill savings recorded were ECU11 per annum. Since 75 per cent of those surveyed were positive about the effects of the scheme, this suggests that up to 80 per cent of the potential savings were taken in increased heat. While these benefits are real, the energy savings are lower than might be expected. Annual actual CO_2 emission reductions are estimated at 0.7 tonnes per household. Applying this to the total recipients to the end of 1993 gives an annual reduction in CO_2 emissions of over 400 000 tonnes. As a footnote, two-thirds of recipients stated that they would not have carried out the work on their dwellings without the grant.

The scheme has a positive employment impact, with approximately 400 approved installers in place. EAGA (1994) claims that there are 1,830 'full-time equivalent staff' employed under the scheme, 20 per cent of whom are in government training programmes. A further 78 staff are employed by EAGA itself. Indirect employment effects would also flow from the manufacture of the insulating materials.

There are also probably some health benefits from the programme, as the pattern of energy savings indicates that previous warmth levels in recipient households were possibly inadequate. These benefits are difficult to quantify, but research on the overall health effects of poor housing in the UK has been carried out. For instance, total extra health costs of ECU380 per inhabitant per year due to adverse housing conditions have been indicated (Hunt and Boardman 1994, p. 30), and Boardman (1991b) states that 'illness that results from condensation and mould in cold homes costs the National Health Service £800 million[8] a year'. A further possible benefit relates to reductions in housing maintenance costs. This was quantified in other programmes aimed specifically at public sector housing, but was not mentioned in the literature for this programme.

In conclusion, the scheme seems to be successful in terms of improving the energy efficiency of low-income households. However, much of the savings are used to purchase more warmth, so the amount of energy saved is quite modest. If energy saving were the only criterion, the scheme would not be viable. Employment is also created, and there are possible health benefits and reductions in maintenance requirements, although these are not quantified.

The Green House Programme

This scheme involved the expenditure of ECU80 million over a period of three years up to 1993–4 to improve the energy efficiency of local authority housing and reduce CO_2 emissions. Among the criteria used were that a decrease in CO_2 emissions of at least 15 per cent must be achieved and that the buildings must have a lifespan of at least 30 years. Projects had to be either 'innovative', involving new approaches to the problem, or 'strategic', that is, part of a well-integrated energy conservation package. Grants of up to 75 per cent were available to local authorities. The aim of the programme was to establish a network of energy efficient demonstration projects which would be the catalysts for a wider programme of schemes undertaken by local authorities. The Department of the Environment funded 100 per cent of monitoring costs, in line with the demonstration function of the programme.

The scheme received 800 applications from local authorities, out of which some 180 were accepted by the end of 1993. A wide variety of projects has been implemented, ranging from the usual insulation projects to communal Combined Heat and Power (CHP) projects. *Ex ante* estimates of the approved schemes indicate average energy savings of 42 per cent and CO_2 emissions reductions of 56 per cent. The estimated aggregate payback period is 7.7 years.

As indicated, monitoring was an important part of the programme, and results have been published for a number of individual projects. Three of these are dealt with here. The first, in York, looked at the viability of installing energy conservation measures in old (1940s and 1950s) houses as part of a general refurbishment package. A pilot project was set up in which four houses were refurbished and the results monitored (see Table 1.6, column (A)). Costs included are the net additions for the energy conservation measures only, which included general insulation, window replacement and heating system installation. The results show a modest return on the investment, with a relatively long payback period. This is interesting, given that the energy conservation work was 'piggy-backed' on general refurbishment work; however, the rate of return is still probably satisfactory. One of the houses in the project had a poorer return than the others in terms of energy saving. It had had an innovative heating system installed with heat recovery and a heat pump, and improper functioning of the heat pump was considered a possible cause of the poor results. This may give an indication of problems when innovative technology is installed in houses.

Table 1.6   The Green House Programme, UK: sample projects

	York (4 houses) (A)	Enfield (64 blocks of flats) (B)	Hove (two blocks of flats) (C)
Year of completion	1992	1992	1992
Total costs (000s 1994 ECU)	20	96	321
Private benefits (annual) (000s 1994 ECU)			
Energy	2	12	23
Non-energy		9	
Total	2	21	23
Private benefits vs total costs			
Net present value (000s 1994 ECU)	11	163	(33)
Internal rate of return (%)	11	21	4
Simple payback (years)	8	4.6	13.9
Energy saving (annual) (TOE)	4	12	17
Public benefits: reductions in emissions (annual) (tonnes)			
CO_2 (tonnes)	16	119	88
Others	unknown	unknown	unknown
Employment effects	positive	positive	positive

Notes:
1. NPV is calculated using a discount rate of 5 per cent.
2. Energy-saving installations are assumed to have a lifespan of 20 years.
3. Only reductions in CO_2 emissions were calculated in these cost-benefit studies.

Source: Department of the Environment.

The second project relates to the replacement of lighting in communal areas in blocks of flats in the London Borough of Enfield. Incandescent lighting was to be replaced by compact fluorescent lamps (CFLs), and 64 buildings, containing 1600 flats, were included. Details are shown in Table 1.6, column (B). The results are quite positive, as might be expected from such a project. Energy savings were lower than anticipated, but this is because much of the savings were used to increase lighting levels, which previously had been inadequate. Had the old lighting system been adequate, the savings from this project would have been significantly greater: the Building Research Energy Conservation Support Unit (BRECSU), which carried out the study of the project, estimated that a payback period of less than one year would have been achieved if this had been the case. Apart from energy, a number of other savings ensued. Maintenance costs were considerably reduced due to the longer life of CFLs. The increased lighting levels enhanced tenants' feeling of security and reduced vandalism (this benefit was not enumerated). BRECSU calculated that if this scheme were extended to the approximately five million public authority dwellings of this type in the UK, reductions in CO_2 emissions of almost 400 000 tonnes per annum could be achieved.

The third project was the comprehensive refurbishment of two blocks of flats (20 flats in all) in Hove, Sussex. This included new heating systems, double glazing, insulation, ventilation with heat recovery in all rooms. Four of the flats were monitored and the results extended to the entire project. The results show a very modest return on the investment – only 4 per cent. This does not appear to justify the scheme in terms of cost of energy saved alone. Monitoring showed that some of the installed devices, especially the ventilation systems, were not well understood by the occupants, and this may have reduced the savings achieved. The monitoring agency recommended that better advice should have been made available to the tenants as part of the project.

Although the detailed monitoring of only three schemes is included here, a number of points can be made:

1. The returns on investment, in terms of the enumerated benefits are modest but probably satisfactory,[9] and seem to agree broadly with the *ex ante* estimated payback period of 7.7 years for the entire Green House Programme.
2. The best return was achieved on the simplest of the three schemes – the light replacement project in Enfield. The more complex schemes appeared to suffer from equipment malfunction or user difficulties, which reduced the savings made. They also had the longest payback period, notwithstanding these problems. This suggests that more straightforward projects should get priority or that more effort be given to user training.
3. Even with the lighting scheme, much of the estimated savings did not materialize, because the old system provided an inadequate level of service.

Hence much of the savings were taken in the form of better service rather than saved energy. This does not invalidate such projects but may highlight problems with levels of service, which may have to be dealt with (though at a cost) independently of the requirement for energy conservation.

In addition to the above, the Department of the Environment (1994), in summarizing the monitoring of 1991–2 Green House projects, made the following points:

1. Advice to tenants is very important; the approach of providing people with energy advice leaflets was found to be 'not sufficiently effective'. The Department suggests training tenants and staff, organizing exhibitions and talks to community groups, better consultation with tenants at the beginning of a project, and collection of and action on feedback at the end of a project as possible ways of improving project effectiveness and user satisfaction.
2. In addition to savings in energy, local authority landlords can achieve other substantial savings from projects. These are in the form of lower maintenance costs, fewer complaints and vandalism, and fewer empty dwellings. Estimated potential local authority savings are ECU130–640 per dwelling per annum due to reduced maintenance and operating costs, apart from energy saving per dwelling of ECU65-130 per annum.[10] It concludes: 'if landlord savings are added to the value of the energy savings, then the payback period can be reduced to a half or even a third of the period for fuel savings alone'.

Employment effects are potentially significant but will vary from project to project, depending on the type of work carried out and equipment installed.

Government Subsidies to the Business Sector

The Energy Management Assistance Scheme
This scheme was introduced in 1992 and was aimed at small businesses (with fewer than 500 employees worldwide), which are responsible for 45 per cent of the energy usage in the UK (National Audit Office, 1994). The scheme was designed to offset the cost of energy consultancy advice. Potential energy savings of at least 10 per cent were required. The scheme has experienced a number of problems, and uptake has used only 30 per cent of the budget. Grants have tended to go to very small businesses and the average level of grant has been much smaller than expected. As a result the budget has been reduced from ECU6.7 million to ECU2.2 million for the current year. The administrators of the scheme believe that the economic recession and the restrictive eligibility criteria were to blame for the low take-up. In particular, many small businesses are subsidiaries of larger companies but operate independently of their parents;

they would not have been eligible for the scheme. A redefinition of these criteria is being considered, but it remains to be seen whether this and the improved economic conditions will increase the effect of the scheme.

Government Investment in Public Sector Buildings

We could find no quantitative analysis of central government investment in energy conservation in public sector buildings in the UK. However, the 'Best Practice' information programme operated by the Department of the Environment does list information on energy conservation programmes in regional health authorities. These data are incomplete, but information on one authority (Somerset Health Authority) which instituted an energy management policy indicates that a payback period of 4–5 years was achieved on capital projects. A 5 per cent reduction in the authority's energy expenditure was achieved; however, good housekeeping – at no capital expense – was equally as effective in reducing expenditure. Qualitative analysis of the policy indicates that management commitment, staff information and training, and the appointment of staff specifically responsible for energy performance were important factors. Information from other hospitals indicates that similar levels of savings are achievable.

In addition, the British National Health Service (NHS) has built two 'low energy hospitals' in the 1990s, one on the Isle of Wight and the other in the north of England, with the aim of reducing consumption by 50 per cent *vis-à-vis* comparable hospitals. Both schemes are the subject of detailed monitoring, and detailed reports have been published on the Isle of Wight scheme (NHS Estates, 1994a and b); some of the results are considered here. By its second year of operation (1993) the hospital was using 44 per cent less energy than an equivalent facility built in the 1990s, giving a saving of 1000 tonnes of CO_2 per annum. In monetary terms this amounted to ECU65 000 per annum, compared with an extra capital cost, due to the energy-saving measures, of ECU1 368 000 and extra maintenance costs of ECU26 000 per annum. These costs and savings give a simple payback period of 35 years. However, the period varied widely for the various measures: from less than two years for lighting to almost 50 years for the space heating measures.

The reports make a number of conclusions:

1. The target saving is ECU128 000 per annum, after the lessons learnt from the first few years of operation are taken into account. Such a saving, if achieved, will obviously improve the viability of the project. The simple payback period would be reduced to 13.4 years, and the NPV would be a positive ECU97 000.[11] Improved housekeeping is listed as the main cause of the further improvement.

2. Low energy prices have had an adverse effect on the viability of the project.
3. The Isle of Wight hospital, being a pilot project, is more expensive and includes certain measures that have turned out to be non-viable. New hospitals will benefit from the lessons learnt; the reports estimate that 'an investment equivalent to 2.5 per cent of the works cost is likely to secure savings of about 50% [in energy costs]'.
4. Applying the conclusions to the whole of the NHS, the reports state that there are approximately 1500 hospitals in England, using 1.4 Million Tonnes of Oil Equipment (MTOE) per annum. If the savings achieved in the Isle of Wight hospital were applied to all of these, savings would exceed 600 000 TOE per annum, representing 2 million tonnes of CO_2 and costs savings of ECU255 million annually.

Conclusion

The bulk of the energy conservation effort in the UK over recent years has centred on the housing sector, mainly on low-income or public housing. Evaluation of the schemes has been incomplete but some tentative conclusions can be drawn. First, low-income households tend to spend most of the savings in the form of increased comfort, thus reducing the energy savings. However, this may result in improved health, which will yield public savings, and, along with increased householder comfort, represent improvements in welfare. Second, the more straightforward projects seem to be the most successful. Complicated or innovative measures tend to have longer payback periods, and may be prone to breakdown or user misunderstanding, thus further reducing the benefit. Third, energy advice which involves simply giving people leaflets does not appear to be adequate. Demonstrations, exhibitions and householder training are recommended as likely to achieve better results. Fourth, older grant schemes, which were open to all households, seem generally to have gone to the better-off; it is not clear which characteristics of these schemes caused this. The newer HEES is aimed exclusively at low-income households, and the grant rate is effectively 100 per cent. Finally, information on hospitals indicates that, as in Ireland, considerable saving can be made on energy usage in this sector as much by good management/housekeeping as by capital investment.

THE NETHERLANDS[12]

Energy conservation in the Dutch housing sector became an issue after the first oil crisis in 1973. Adequate insulation, especially in the older stock, was seen as a prime target. A number of schemes have been put in place since then. While we have not been able to obtain cost-benefit analyses for them, some qualitative information is available. A description of the various schemes is given, along with some of the related findings.

From 1974 to 1979 there were grants for insulation for all housing. In 1979 the National Insulation Programme (NIP) was initiated. From this year also, grants were restricted to existing houses, new houses being covered by mandatory insulation standards. The programme initially set a target of 2.5 million houses to be insulated over ten years. The government decided to set their target at 200 000 houses per annum, with a maximum subsidy of ECU850[13] per dwelling to cover double glazing and the insulation of cavity walls, floors and roofs. Later, subsidies were made available for installations and regulation systems (for example, thermostats, new boilers, and so on). The NIP continued until 1988 in this format.

In 1982 it became clear that grants were going predominantly to owner-occupiers. The rented sector was not reacting to the incentives.[14] Tenants had to agree to the improvements and rents would be increased automatically as a result, so it was difficult to convince them that such improvements would be to their benefit. As a result of this finding, grants to the rented sector were increased so that rents would need to increase by less as a result of energy conservation investment by landlords, and grants to owner-occupiers were abolished.

From 1987 the grant scheme became a house improvement scheme – energy-conservation measures would only be grant-aided if they were part of a general home improvement scheme. At the moment grants are available under two schemes (to those in rented accommodation only):

1. Energy conservation in existing buildings   This scheme pays a fixed amount per cubic metre for insulation and double glazing (ECU3–33 per m^3) or 25 per cent of the overall cost. The budget for 1992 and 1993 was ECU62 million per annum (50 per cent each from the government and the energy distribution companies). The budget was not fully spent in 1992; although the reason for this is not given, it may reflect continuing problems with encouraging energy conservation in rented accommodation.
2. High-efficiency and low-emission central heating boilers   This scheme pays ECU3–5 per kW of capacity for new boilers installed (the usual grant is ECU95–160 per boiler) and has proved to be very popular: the entire budget of ECU12 million for 1993 had been spent by mid-year (funded 60:40 from the government and the energy companies). The pattern of uptake is very interesting; in 1991, 95 000 new boilers were sold, but there were few applications for grants. In 1992, 120 000 boilers were sold, of which half were grant-aided. By mid-1993, as many grants had been paid as in the whole of 1992 (though the number of boilers sold is not given). The scheme is to be dropped in 1994.

Evidence suggests that, over time, people are requiring ever greater degrees of comfort in their houses. This means higher internal temperatures and more rooms being heated. This obviously counteracts the benefits from better insulation and other energy-conserving measures. De Paauw and Kaan (1994) call this the 'rebound effect' whereby, because of increased energy efficiency in houses, a greater level of heat can be enjoyed without increased cost. It seems to suggest that even among better-off households the amount of actual energy-saving that can be achieved in the home may be limited. However, this observation may simply reflect low energy prices in recent years; it would be interesting to see the effect of a price increase on this trend. None the less, this does not necessarily invalidate energy-saving measures: it may be that people would have sought higher comfort levels anyway, with the result that energy usage would have been even greater without the energy conservation measures.

Because of the problems found with energy conservation in the rented sector, the government is trying to encourage more owner-occupation of dwellings among low-income groups, as owner-occupiers appear more likely to install energy conservation measures. Also 'graduated rent subsidies' have been introduced to cushion the effects of rent increases in the year after renovations. We could find no evaluations of these schemes.

Conclusion

While no cost-benefit analyses have been found of Dutch schemes, some qualitative conclusions have been made. First, most grants in earlier schemes seem to have gone to owner-occupiers, who are presumably better-off. The Dutch system explicitly allows landlords to increase rents as a result of improvements to dwellings, but they must get tenants' permission for the improvements first. The rent increases overcome the landlords' problem with energy conservation in rented dwellings, but at the same time they make it more difficult to convince tenants of the benefits. Second, householders are seeking ever greater levels of comfort in their dwellings, and this appears to apply to the better-off as well as to low-income households. This suggests that reducing energy usage in the household sector in the future may be problematic; greater energy efficiency may be needed simply to stabilize usage. This also has implications for achieving emission reductions in the domestic sector.

GERMANY

German government energy policy has been based on the premise that intervention is only justified to correct a market failure. The most recent quantitative data on energy conservation grants and subsidies in Germany date from 1982 (IFO, 1982; ISI, 1982). This dealt with, *inter alia*, a Dm4.35 billion grant programme for energy saving in dwellings, known as the *Bund-Länder-Programm* or the *4.35 Billion DM Programm*, which we now examine.

This major programme ran from mid-1978 to mid-1983 and involved a grant and a tax allowance (recipients could claim one or the other). The grant covered 25 per cent of the investment cost for ECU3000–9000 of investment per dwelling. The tax allowance amounted to 10 per cent of investment cost for ten years (normally 2–5 per cent would be allowed). The work covered was insulation and improvements in heating systems for houses built before 1978, and innovative heating systems (for example, heat recovery systems, solar appliances, and so on) for all houses. The budget was ECU1.84 billion in grants and ECU1.58 billion for tax relief, giving a total of ECU3.42 billion. Participation was 1.51 million dwellings for grants and 0.92 million dwellings for tax relief. The incentives were available to owners only.

The grant budget was completely taken up, with the vast majority of recipients (over 90 per cent) using it for improved insulation – 77 per cent for double glazing alone. Only a very small proportion went on innovative technology.[15] The average grant was ECU1100, indicating an average investment of ECU4400. Total investment was ECU18–19 billion, and the expected fuel savings were 2.42 MTOE per annum (mainly on heating oil and gas). This points to a cost saving of roughly ECU800 million per annum and a payback period of over 20 years.[16] On this basis the project was not cost-effective. We could not find any analysis of the reasons for such poor results, but the fact that a large proportion of the investment was spent on installing double-glazing may have been a factor.[17]

External benefits are in the form of reduced emissions – approximately 6 million tonnes of CO_2 per annum. Positive employment effects also flowed from the scheme, but are not quantified.

DENMARK

We could obtain no cost-benefit analyses of energy conservation programmes in Denmark, but the qualitative information which was available is given here. Denmark's first grant programme for energy conservation in the housing sector ran from 1975 to 1980. It gave a grant of 20–35 per cent, up to a maximum of ECU690 per dwelling. A total of ECU0.52 billion was dispersed, stimulating approximately ECU1.72 billion in investment. However, it appears that this did not have the desired energy-saving effect, because 'people used the grants primarily for retrofits of walls and windows, which produced cosmetic rather than thermal improvements' (Wilson *et al.*, 1989). This experience prompted the government to restrict the grants to a specific list of investments. Between 1978 and 1980 there also existed a tax-deduction scheme for energy-saving retrofits; however, take-up was 'much lower than expected, possibly because of the time lapse between the actual expenditure and the related tax savings' (ISI 1982, quoted in Wilson *et al.*, 1989).

In 1980 these schemes were replaced with two grant schemes, the first aimed at energy conservation in general and the second at energy conservation and/or improvements in buildings. The maximum grant was increased to ECU1530 per dwelling (more than double the previous level). No evaluation of these schemes is available, but the entire grant fund of ECU153 million for the two schemes was exhausted in 4.5 months. Wilson *et al.* (1989) surmise that this may reflect that higher absolute levels of grants are more attractive to householders. It appears that since the mid-1980s the main method of encouraging energy conservation in Denmark has been through energy taxes, which have counteracted the reductions in energy prices.

SUMMARY AND RECOMMENDATIONS

This chapter has examined the costs and benefits of subsidies and investments by governments to improve the energy efficiency of heating and insulation systems in buildings. It has considered schemes in a number of countries and drawn conclusions from the results. Many of these conclusions are qualitative in nature, reflecting the lack of quantitative cost-benefit analysis of schemes in all the countries examined. This prevents giving a more robust answer to the question of the effectiveness of energy conservation measures. Given the amount of funds allocated to these measures, it seems strange that more effort has not gone into their evaluation, since it would be expected to yield valuable information to policy-makers. However, it seems that the difficulty of evaluation,[18] and perhaps a lack of incentive for the energy agencies to carry out evaluation,[19] may be factors. This lack of evaluation, which is not uncommon in other areas, should be addressed.

Notwithstanding this, some conclusions can be drawn, and these are summarized here. This is followed by policy recommendations arising from these conclusions.

Conclusions

1. In Ireland to date, there has been a general lack of investment by the government in energy conservation. This is especially true with respect to the public sector, where budgeting procedures and restrictions on borrowing

have combined to deprive managers of the means and the incentive to introduce energy-saving measures. This is despite the results of pilot projects which have shown that considerable savings and short payback periods can be achieved in the case of investment in office buildings, and even more so in the case of hospitals. The recent increase in the budget for energy conservation should bring about substantial improvements.

2. Information from Ireland and the UK indicates that there is much potential for energy conservation in the hospital sector. In Ireland, a major reason for this has been the use of inefficient heating systems. In the UK, increasing energy intensity in recent years is a factor (this may also be relevant in continental European countries). Quite apart from capital investments, good housekeeping has been found to be very effective in reducing energy consumption in this sector.

3. In both Ireland and the UK, the need for energy conservation in low-income households was apparent.[20] This was due to the combination of poor insulation standards and inefficient heating systems and might suggest that there is more scope for energy conservation in this sector. However, evidence from the UK showed that attempts to reduce energy usage in this sector were problematic, because much of the savings were taken in the form of increased heat. The implication is that these households were inadequately heated in the first place, and research from Ireland and the UK lends weight to this hypothesis. This means that little energy would be saved *per se* by schemes aimed at this sector. However, other benefits, such as improved health and greater comfort, would flow from such schemes and would benefit society.

4. Evidence from the UK also suggests that schemes involving more innovative or complex devices in the housing sector, and with longer payback periods, may be prone to improper use and breakdown. This obviously reduces their effectiveness. The implication is that simpler measures which householders can understand and operate properly are more likely to succeed and deliver the estimated benefits. On a related theme, experience of UK schemes indicated that energy advice needs to be more comprehensive than simply sending householders leaflets through the post. Householder training, demonstrations, and so on are recommended as being more effective.

5. Evidence from the UK and the Netherlands indicates that grants for house improvements have generally gone to higher-income households and owner-occupiers. This may be seen as undesirable, since such householders should in theory be able to afford to invest in viable, energy-saving measures without the need for a grant. (In fact, the points made in 3 above might indicate that more energy savings could be achieved from conservation by the better-off, but see 7 below.) Energy conservation in the rented sector in particular seems to be problematic, due to:

(a) low income of tenants, and their reluctance to invest in property they do not own;

(b) the inability of landlords to pass on the cost of energy-saving investment, or conversely, their ability to pass on energy price increases where heating is included in the rent;[21]

(c) where there is no individual metering and billing of tenants, the difficulty for tenants of capturing the benefits of energy conservation.

In the Netherlands poor grant uptake among lower-income households may be related to the fact that improvements to accommodation are automatically reflected in the rent but can only be carried out with the tenant's permission. The adjustment to rent presumably gets over the problems of convincing landlords to invest in the improvement of their properties, but makes it difficult to convince tenants to agree to such improvements. In both the UK and the Netherlands grants have been adjusted to become more focused on low-income or rented accommodation.

6. Findings in Ireland and Denmark suggest that the absolute amount of the grant is a big determinant of its take-up among householders. This may reflect the fact that grants tend to be taken up by middle- to high-income households, and that large grants are more attractive to these groups.

7. Dutch studies have indicated that over time householders in general are demanding greater levels of heat and comfort, regardless of income level. Also, in a number of countries a trend towards an increase in the number of households, each with a smaller number of occupants, has been noted. If these trends are generalized, it increases the challenge of achieving reductions in household energy usage. However, it does not invalidate energy conservation measures for households, since it may be that in the absence of such measures energy usage in the sector would increase significantly.

8. In a number of the countries we looked at, grant schemes to the household sector suffered from a lack of precision, in that the type of allowable expenditure was not sufficiently tightly defined to encourage investment in genuinely energy-saving measures. As a result, in many cases householders used the grants to finance measures which did not improve energy efficiency. However, grant schemes which are confined to genuinely energy-saving measures can be successful.

9. Finally, the fall in energy prices since the mid-1980s has perhaps blunted the urgency of energy conservation in the minds of householders and governments. More recently, the threat of global warming has changed this somewhat, although the lack of incentive for households due to low energy prices may make it difficult to convert this change into action.

Policy Recommendations

What are the policy implications for government investments and subsidies in the area of energy conservation? The following points can be made:

1. In Ireland, more central government funding of energy conservation in the public sector and more flexible budgeting arrangements in the public sector are needed, if the potential for saving energy in this sector is to be achieved.[22] However, the government needs to be mindful of lessons to be learnt from other countries' experience. Office buildings and the health sector appear to offer particularly good potential. This may well be reflected in other countries.
2. Grants and subsidies to the household sector are problematic, in that they often seem to go predominantly to better-off people who do not need them, and they are often spent on measures which have little effect on energy usage. By the same token, savings from improvements to lower-income dwellings are largely used to purchase more energy, albeit while achieving other benefits. Therefore, if they are to be used, such schemes need to be carefully designed, in terms of the target population, its works to be aided, and the hoped-for benefits. The following points are relevant:

   (a) large grants stimulate a bigger response than small ones, but may attract more high-income beneficiaries;
   (b) grants should only be given for genuinely energy-saving measures: for example, double-glazing is a popular investment which has only minor energy conservation benefits;
   (c) the rented sector, while having large potential energy savings, is very difficult to target; measures need to benefit both landlord and tenant to be successful.

   It may be that energy conservation schemes in the household sector will only hold energy usage at current levels, rather than bring about a large reduction. This may justify such schemes, however, if energy usage would have increased significantly in their absence.
3. There appears to be considerable potential benefit from schemes such as Energy Action in Ireland and the larger-scale HEES in the UK which aid the installation of basic energy conservation measures in low-income households. Such schemes will undoubtedly yield benefits to society, but perhaps more in terms of greater comfort, better health and possibly employment creation than in reduced energy usage.
4. Programmes focused on innovative or novel technologies are more prone to failure than those involving well-proven and straightforward measures. This is especially true in the domestic sector, where it may be that initiatives involving such technologies should be restricted to pilot schemes at this stage.

5. Publicity and information campaigns need to be more interactive with potential beneficiaries. Leaflets through the letterbox are generally ignored, and the same may be true of TV and radio advertising. Demonstrations, exhibitions and personal contact with potential beneficiaries are likely to be more successful. Once again, this applies especially to the household sector, where poor understanding of household appliances and energy-saving installations appears to pose problems.

6. As already stated, inadequate evaluation of energy conservation programmes appears to be a widespread phenomenon. This hampers any attempt to identify the programmes which are successful and those which are failures, and the reasons for this. Given the resources invested in this area, proper evaluation is essential and should be explicitly built into the operation and budgets of all such programmes.

7. Finally, as already stated, low energy prices in recent years may have reduced the incentive to conserve energy. Perhaps an energy or carbon tax, as used in Denmark and other Scandinavian countries, may be appropriate in addition to grants and government investment, to counteract the effects of low energy prices.

APPENDIX 1: EXCHANGE RATES, DISCOUNT RATES AND INFLATION INDICES USED

Unless otherwise stated, all values are in 1994 ECUs. The inflation indices used are published energy price indices for fuels and consumer/retail price indices for other items. Because of falling real fuel prices in recent years, this produces different payback periods, net present values and so on, than if the same indices were used for costs and energy savings. While in some cases the difference is significant, in all cases examined in this chapter the overall evaluation is robust as between the different indexation approaches. The discount rate used for calculating net present value is 5 per cent. The exchange rates used are given in Table A1.1

Table A1.1   Exchange rates

National currency	ECUs equivalent
Irish £	1.265
UK £	1.276
Netherlands florin	0.469
German D-mark	0.527
Danish krone	0.134

APPENDIX 2: CONVERSION FACTORS

Table A1.2   Conversion factors for individual fuels to tonnes of oil equivalent (TOE) and to emissions

Fuel type	Unit	TOE per unit	Tonnes of emissions per TOE				
			CO_2	NO_x	SO_2	VOC	CO
Coal	tonne	0.6650	3.70	0.0021	0.0241	0.0105	0.0676
Loose turf	tonne	0.3130	4.34	0.0042	0.0126	0.0042	0.0732
Central heating oil/gas oil	tonne	1.0334	3.05	0.0021	0.0059	0.0004	0.0007
Heavy fuel oil	tonne	0.9849	3.18	0.005	0.0527	0	0.0005
Liquid and propane gas	tonne	1.1263	2.67	0.0021	0	0	0.0004
Electricity	1000 kWh	0.2650	10.26	0.0438	0.0973	0.0002	0.0031
Natural gas	1000 therms	2.4398	2.07	0.0021	0	0.0002	0.0004

Notes:
1. 1 TOE = 10^7 kilocalories = 41.84 Gj.
2. The TOE for electricity represents the figure at generation.
3. 1 therm of gas = $2.735m^3$.

Sources: Scott (1992, pp. 21–34); McGettigan,1993, pp. 14–15).

APPENDIX 3: MONETARY VALUATION OF EXTERNAL COSTS OF ENERGY USAGE

The monetary valuation of external costs is a difficult and controversial task. For the purposes of this chapter I have used information from CEPN *et al.* (1994), an extract from which appears at the end of this appendix. The CEPN report attempts to value the external costs of generating electricity from various fuels: fossil, nuclear and renewable. The extract deals only with fossil fuels and, as can be seen, a number of damage categories are either not valued or only partly valued. In addition, it only deals with six specific power stations burning specific fuels, so the results may not be generalizable. Most importantly, global warming effects are not dealt with at all in the report, although there is a literature review of this area, and the results of other studies are summarized. The CEPN report also summarizes costs from the nuclear and renewable fuel cycles, but these are equally incomplete and I have not used them.

Subject to all these provisos, I have taken external costs from the extract, as follows. With respect to the non-global warming costs, I have used Table 6.1 in the extract and averaged the quantified costs across the six examples. The global warming costs, reviewed in Table 6.2, contain one further complication in that the range of costs is enormous. I have used the lowest cost estimate (from Fankhauser, 1993) and taken the average across the different fuel cycles. The resulting estimate of damage costs is as follows (mECUs are milli-ECUs or thousandths of ECUs):

	mECU/kWh
Average non-global warming damage costs	9
Global warming damage costs	8
Total	17

This may be a conservative estimate of the external costs, as the estimate of non-global warming costs is incomplete and that of global warming costs is the lowest of those reviewed by CEPN. The next step is to apply these costs to the energy savings achieved in the various projects referred to in this chapter. This raises one further problem in that the above figures relate to electricity generation, whereas many of the projects reviewed here involve other fuels. To deal with this I have converted electricity generation into tonnes of oil equivalent (TOE) required as input, at a rate of 3.773 kWh = 1 TOE (as in Appendix II). This is very far from being satisfactory, but it is the best available approach. At this rate the use of one TOE will entail external costs of ECU64.

Table A1.3   Evaluation of energy-saving programmes, taking into account internal and external costs

Programme	Country	TOE saved annually	Annual external costs avoided due to energy saving (ECU '000)	Evaluation of programme taking into account internal and external costs		
				NPV[a] (ECU '000)	IRR[b] (%)	Simple payback (years)
Attic insulation grants	Ireland	10 600	680	32 346	35	2.8
Energy Action (ref. Table 1.1)	Ireland	83	5	834	41	2.4
Energy Action (ref. Table 1.2)	Ireland	83	5	743	31	3.1
Office buildings	Ireland	35	2	131	32	3.0
Hospitals (A)	Ireland	815	52	4 431	62	1.6
Hospitals (B)	Ireland	393	25	3 644	159	0.7
Hospitals (C)	Ireland	132	8	823	134	0.7
Green House (A)	UK	4	0.3	15	13	7.2
Green House (B)	UK	12	1	173	22	4.4
Green House (C)	UK	17	1	(20)	4	13.3
Bund-Länder-Programm	Germany	2 420 000	155 000	(6 596 000)	0	19.0

Notes:
[a] NPV = net present value.
[b] IRR = internal rate of return.

The point of interest in this exercise is whether the inclusion of external costs will be critical in determining whether a particular energy conservation programme is worthwhile. In other words, whether a programme which was rejected as non-viable on purely market-based criteria would be viable if external benefits were included. In the context of the programmes reviewed in this chapter, the answer in general is no, as Table A1.3 indicates. This is perhaps not surprising, since most of the programmes reviewed were either clear-cut successes or failures. One could envisage programmes where the external costs would be critical; however, one might conclude that the inclusion of external costs at the levels calculated above would at most turn a marginally non-viable programme into a marginally viable one. Higher estimates of external costs, as might be valid given the limitations in the CEPN report, might give a different result.

Table A1.4   Damage estimates from the ExternE project for the main fossil fuel cycles

| Damage category | Valuation estimate (mECU/kWh) | | | | | |
| | Coal | | Lignite | Oil | | Gas |
	UK	Germany	Germany	GT	CCGT	UK
Public health	4[a]	13	10	11	10	0.5[a]
Occupational health						
diseases	0.1	0.3	neg.	neg.	neg.	neg.
accidents	0.8	2.0	0.1	0.5	0.3	0.1
Agriculture	0.03	0.04	0.02	0.04	0.03	NQ
Timber	0.004	IQ	0.004	0.013	0.009	neg.
Terrestrial ecosystems	NQ	NQ	NQ	NQ	NQ	NQ
Marine ecosystems	NQ	NQ	NQ	0.2	0.2	0.001
Fisheries	IQ	NQ	NQ	NQ	NQ	NQ
Materials	1.3	0.1	0.1	0.2	0.1	0.1
Noise	0.2	NQ	NQ	NQ	NQ	0.03
Other impacts	NQ	NQ	NQ	NQ	NQ	NQ
Sub-total	6[a]	15	10	12	11	0.8[a]
Total	NQ	NQ	NQ	NQ	NQ	NQ

Notes:
NQ = not quantified within this report, though some discussion of effects is given.
IQ = impacts have been quantified but nor yet valued.
neg. = negligible.
[a] Public health impact assessed over the UK only.

Source: CEPN *et al.* (1994, p. 161).

Table A1.5   *Review of global warming damage estimates*

Source	Valuation estimate (mECU/kWh)			
	Coal	lignite	Oil CC	Gas
Cline (1992)	15	19	10	6
Fankhauser (1993)	10	12	6	4
Tol 1995[a]	18	22	12	8
Hohmeyer and Gärtner (1992)	5000	6200	3200	2100

Note: [a]
Figures based on Tol (1995) use a 1 per cent discount rate.

Source: As Table A1.4.

NOTES

1. Paradoxically, the suggested rate of return on public capital projects appears to be 5 per cent real (Department of Finance, 1984). However, tight budgetary controls have made it exceedingly difficult to obtain finance for such projects.
2. An information campaign, informing the public of the economic viability of energy conservation might be more effective for middle- to upper-income groups.
3. Throughout this chapter 'free rider' will be used to describe people who avail themselves of a grant or subsidy who would have undertaken the grant-aided activity anyway.
4. The scheme has been in place since 1987; total expenditure to 1994 has been over ECU800,000.
5. 1 tonne of oil equivalent (TOE) = 41.84Gj.
6. A large part of the work over the last decade and a half has been carried out by a network of 300 local energy projects, similar to the one described in Ireland, co-ordinated by a national charity – Neighbourhood Energy Action. The largest of these is Heatwise Glasgow in Scotland, which has worked on over 70 000 low-income households in the city of Glasgow.
7. This evaluation was not published and it is not clear whether administration costs or beneficiary contributions were included in the payback calculation.
8. Equal to ECU1.02 billion.
9. Assuming that more worthwhile projects were not displaced by this one. Setting the appropriate rate of return for public projects is controversial. The required rate of return assumed in this chapter is 5 per cent real.
10. The makeup of these figures is not given.
11. Given a 5 per cent discount rate and a 20-year life.
12. This section draws extensively on De Paauw and Kaan (1994).
13. Based on grant level in 1979.
14. Public sector housing and housing associations own 42 per cent of the housing stock in the Netherlands.
15. These data refer to take-up in 1979.
16. Assuming a 20-year lifespan for work carried out and a discount rate of 5 per cent, net present value for the programme is ECU8.5 billion negative.
17. IFO (1982) points to some criticism of the scheme on the basis that it grant-aided window replacement which would have happened anyway. This is not backed up with research findings, but to the degree that this occurred it would have further reduced the effectiveness of the scheme.

18. 'Before and after' monitoring of energy consumption in the domestic sector appears to be particularly difficult, due to variability in climate and to household habits, size, purchases, income, and so on.
19. 'One of the most significant institutional barriers to program evaluations is the fear of annihilation' (Wilson *et al.*, 1989).
20. This mirrors the situation in other countries, such as the Netherlands, in the past.
21. Wilson *et al.* (1989) note that in Sweden this was addressed by preventing landlords from passing on the full cost of energy price increases in rents. This gave them a strong incentive to increase the energy efficiency of their buildings.
22. As stated, the Irish government has already substantially increased its budgeted expenditure in this area.

REFERENCES

Biger, G. and G. Olive (1993), *Mesures d'obligation et d'incitation pour la maîtrise de l'energie dans les bâtiments en France* [Mandatory and Economic Measures for the Control of Energy in Buildings in France], Paris: Bureau d'Études Gilles Olive (BEGO).

Boardman, B. (1990), *Fuel Poverty and the Greenhouse Effect*, London: Neighbourhood Energy Action, Heatwise Glasgow, National Right to Fuel Campaign, and Friends of the Earth.

Boardman, B. (1991a), *Fuel Poverty*, London: Belhaven Press.

Boardman, B. (1991b), 'Fuel poverty is different', *Policy Studies*, **12**(4), 30–41.

Brabazon, P. (1992), 'Retrofit lighting scheme at the Department of Energy', paper given at 'New Energy Technologies for Commercial and Public Sector Buildings', 21 October, Dublin.

Brabazon, P. and E. Connolly (1991), 'Energy audits at Department of Energy buildings at Clare Street and Beggar's Bush', report by EOLAS for the Department of Energy, unpublished.

Centre d'Étude sur l'Évaluation de la Protection de la Domaine Nucleaire (CEPN) ETSU, Ecole des Mines, IER and Metroeconomica (1994), *Externalities of Fuel Cycles: ExternE Project, Summary Report*, Brussels: European Commission, DG XII.

Centre for European Policy Studies (1994), *Policies for Energy Efficiency: A Cost Effective Approach to Environmental Concerns*, Working Party Report no. 10, Brussels: CEPS.

Cline, W. R. (1992), *The Economics of Global Warming*, Washington, DC: Institute for International Economics.

Condon, T. (1985), *Energy Use in Health Buildings*, Strasbourg: Council of Europe.

Condon, T. (1994), Personal communication.

Deering, D. (1989), 'Organising an energy management programme in a health board', Department of Health, unpublished.

De Paauw, K. and H. Kaan (1994), *Energy Conservation Policy in the Dutch Housing Sector*, ECN Project no. 7099, Petten, Netherlands (mimeo).

Department of the Environment (UK) (1992), *Good Practice Case Study: Energy Savings in Hospitals* (GPG 129), Energy Efficiency Office Best Practice Programme, London: DOE.

Department of the Environment (UK) (1993), *Good Practice Case Study: Reducing Electricity Consumption and Costs in Hospitals* (GPG 130), Energy Efficiency Office Best Practice Programme, London: DOE.

Department of the Environment (UK) (1994), 'Monitoring of flagship schemes', *DOE Green House Action*, no. 11, February.

Department of Finance (1984), *Budget 1984*, Dublin: Stationery Office.

Fankhauser, S. (1993), *Global Warming Damage Costs – Some Monetary Estimates*, CSERGE GEC Working Paper 92–129, Norwich: University of East Anglia.

Government of Ireland (1991), *Census 86*, vol. 3: *Household Composition and Family Units*, Dublin: Stationery Office.

Hohmeyer, O. and M. Gärtner (1992), *The Costs of Climate Change*, Karlsruhe: Fraunhofer Institut für Systemtechnik und Innovationforschung.

Hunt, S. and B. Boardman (1994), 'Defining the problem', in Markus, T.A. (ed.), *Domestic Energy and Affordable Warmth*, Watt Committee on Energy Report no. 30, London: E. and F.N. Spon, 17–32.

Institut für Wirtschaftsforschung (IFO) (1982), *Abschätzung der Quantitativen Wirkung von Energieeinsparmaßnahmen – Möglichkeiten und Grenzen* [Assessment of the Quantitative Effects of Energy Saving Measures. Possibilities and Limits], Report for the Federal Ministry of Economics, available from IFO (mimeo).

Irish Energy Centre (1997), *Energy Advisory Board Annual Report*, 1996, Dublin: Irish Energy Centre.

ISI: Fraunhofer Institut für Systemtechnik und Innovationsforschung (1982), *Evaluation of Energy Conservation Programmes in the EC Countries*, study prepared for the Commission of the European Communities DG XVIII (contract no. XVIII/AR/82/264), published subsequently as a Communication from the EU Commission to the Council, under the title 'Comparison of energy saving programmes of the EU member states', Brussels, 2nd February 1984, Com(84)36 final.

Kelly, S. and B. O'Neill (1994), 'A report into the usage of energy in the domestic environment', Dublin: Energy Action, unpublished.

Lowndes, F. (1994), Personal communication.

McGettigan, M. (1993), *CORINAIR 1990 Emissions Inventory for Ireland*, Environmental Research Unit, available from the Environmental Protection Agency, Wexford, Ireland.

McSharry, B. (1993), 'Energy conservation and the domestic sector in the Republic of Ireland', Master's thesis, unpublished.

National Audit Office (1994), *Buildings and the Environment*, London: HMSO.

National Health Service Estates (1991), *A Strategic Guide to Energy Management for General Managers and Chief Executives*, Leeds: NHSE.

National Health Service Estates (1994a), *Low Energy Hospitals: St Mary's Hospital, Isle of Wight, 1st Year Appraisal*, Leeds: NHSE.

National Health Service Estates (1994b), *Low Energy Hospitals: St Mary's Hospital, Isle of Wight, 2nd Year Appraisal*, Leeds: NHSE.

Office of Public Works (1993), *Annual Report 1992*, Dublin: Government Stationery Office.

O'Malley, E. (1990), 'Energy use survey in Irish hospitals', EOLAS, unpublished.

Scott, S. (1992), 'Theoretical considerations and estimates of the effects on households', in J. Fitz Gerald and D. McCoy (eds), *The Economic Effects of Carbon Taxes*, ESRI Policy Research Series Paper no. 14, Dublin: Economic and Social Research Institute.

Sheldrick, B. (1994), 'What price warm, dry, and affordable to heat homes?', paper presented at the 'Energy and the Environment and Environmental Assessment' Conference, Edinburgh, 23 June.

Tol, R.S.J. (1995), *The Damage Costs of Global Warming* Emissions in 'The Dutch Fuel Cycle', ExternE project report to be published, Brussels: the European Commission (DGXII).

Whelan, G. (1994), Personal communication.

Wilson, D., L. Schipper, S. Tyler and S. Bartlett (1989), *Policies and Programs for Promoting Energy Conservation in the Residential Sector: Lessons from Five OECD Countries*, Berkeley (LBL-27289), CA: Lawrence Berkeley Laboratory.

2. Information and consultation: the German experience

Edelgard Gruber

SITUATION AND OBJECTIVES

About one-third of total energy consumption is used for heating buildings; in private households 80 per cent is used for this purpose. Eighty per cent of all buildings were constructed before the first insulation law was in force, and only 1 per cent per year is new build. There is therefore a high potential for energy conservation in Germany, and the main emphasis of energy policy has been in this area. The decision as to which are the correct conservation measures to take, however, is a big problem for many consumers. Federal and regional governments, therefore, promote the instrument of information and consultation.

Energy policy in Germany falls under the competence of the Federal Ministry of Economics and the related Ministries of the Länder governments. Funds for general information programmes and publicity campaigns at the federal level have been greatly reduced and subsidies for investments in private households cut, so information and consultation programmes have been implemented mainly at the regional and local levels. Some Länder pursue the policy of information, motivation, advising and training in a very active manner, for example Northrhine-Westfalia, Saarland, Schleswig-Holstein and Hessen (see Jochem *et al.*, 1996, p. 65). They carry out their own programmes to promote energy consultation. In Northrhine Westfalia, 12 full-time consultants are paid additionally by the regional government (this programme has not been evaluated up to now), and in Hessen three pilot programmes with different kinds of energy consultation were carried out between 1987 and 1992.

Several evaluation studies have been done in order to analyse the benefits of the various programmes (Clausnitzer and Sagehorn 1994). The main results are summarized in this chapter. Some of the results were used to improve the programmes. For comparison, experience of programmes in Denmark will be described.

EVALUATION OF ENERGY CONSULTATION PROGRAMMES FOR PRIVATE HOUSEHOLDS IN GERMANY

Programmes of the Federal Ministry of Economics: Advice centres and audits

At federal level the most important measure in Germany regarding energy consultation programmes for private households are the drop-in advice centres of the consumer organizations (Commission of the European Communities, 1984, p. 103; IFo, ISI, 1990, p. 21). These centres have existed for a long time, but since 1978 energy consultation had been introduced as a special activity. The centres are completely financed by the federal and regional governments. They are available in many cities, the advice is free and the consultants are independent experts working on a part-time basis. Between 1982 and 1992 the number of consultations doubled and expenditure increased from ECU970 000 to ECU2.8 million. An additional ECU500 000 was spent in 1992 on mobile activities (energy buses), which have existed since 1982 and are even more important in the eastern German regions.

Since September 1991, the Federal Ministry of Economics has provided another consultation option, namely, financial incentives to houseowners, landlords and tenants to obtain 'on the spot' consultations, that is a personal visit to the dwelling by an architect or engineer. Up to 95 per cent of the consultation costs are refunded by the Ministry (for example, ECU450 of a maximum ECU475 in one- or two-family houses, ECU800 of a maximum ECU2000 in houses with more than 60 apartments). A prerequisite is that the house must have been built before 1984; the application for the subsidy has to be made by the consultant. In 1991, 440 audits were carried out and 3261 in 1992. The programme finished at the end of 1995. It was tested on a pilot basis in 1988–9, and the findings have been evaluated. The results in terms of costs and benefits were quite positive: an average theoretical energy conservation potential of about 40 per cent was found and a ratio of investment costs to energy savings of about ECU0.50 per kWh saved (GIS, 1990) was achieved. The audit programme addresses a particular target group: more of the clients come from higher-income groups than the visitors to the advice centres, which are discussed below.

Evaluations show that the advice centres are well-known and accepted (Gruber 1992, p. 122). Over time the discussions and recommendations have become more and more specific and detailed. The visitors are very satisfied with the advice and, in many cases (assessments show about two-thirds), follow the suggestions. However, the main reasons for coming to an advice centre are the need to replace an old boiler and the intention to replace old windows. The households often have a certain course of action in mind which they want to have confirmed by the consultant. As far as the insulation standard is concerned, the expert would find it difficult to judge the situation without a personal inspection.

In 1994, Ifo (Institute for Economic Research) carried out an evaluation of the programmes of the Federal Ministry of Economics. On the basis of a representative telephone survey of 3000 households in West Germany, the use of the programmes, the energy conservation investments undertaken and behavioural changes were analysed. Only 27 households out of this sample said that they had had an audit of their house which was subsidized by the government. As this small number did not allow conclusions to be made for the audit programme, 648 users of the programme received a questionnaire; 36 per cent of them have answered.

Of all the households surveyed, 5 per cent have used the advice centres at least once. These households have carried out more energy-saving investments and have saved more energy than the average household in Germany. The author of the evaluation study (Karl, 1994, p. 100) attributes about a 1 per cent saving of household energy consumption to this programme. Table 2.1 shows the influence of consultation on investment and behaviour based on the answers of the respondents.

In the case of personal audits, it is assumed that the report of the consultant includes a cost-efficient energy conservation plan for the building and the heating system. According to the recommendations made, households have the potential to save about 40 per cent of their energy consumption. As they did not undertake all of the suggested measures, their actual potential saving was 25 per cent.

Table 2.1   Influence of recommendations on households' decisions: percentage of recommendations which were acted upon

	Advice centres (%)	Energy buses (%)	Personal audits (%)
Investments			
New windows	55	54	57
Wall insulation	51	81	—
Roof insulation	58	—	41
Cellar ceiling insulation	49	—	—
New heating equipment	50	57	53
Renewable energies	—	—	—
Behavioural change			
Lower room temperature	46	68	46
Ventilation control	36	62	55

This programme is not yet well known or used. One problem is that the cost limit for receiving the grant is regarded as being too low for complete analysis. The author therefore recommends that a short basic audit be given 100 per cent subsidy and that the households finance the whole of a more detailed analysis, if one is justified by the initial basic audit.

Comparative Analysis of Pilot Programmes in Hessen

In Hessen, there exists a very strong and systematic energy conservation policy with many programmes which work together and ensure high efficiency. In this framework three different forms of consultation have been tested: written advice, personal audits and consultation by chimney-sweeps.

Written advice

In the framework of local energy planning in the Vogelsbergkreis region a questionnaire was distributed to households through the official local bulletin. Houseowners were asked to fill in data on building characteristics and heating equipment. An engineering company analysed the data with the help of a computer program and gave written advice to the households. The whole process was free of charge to the households and supported by a certain amount of public-relations activities such as articles in newspapers, exhibitions and so on. The advice included a detailed report on the result of the analysis and recommendations for cost-efficient energy conservation measures.

Personal audits

Special subsidies were granted for audits which had to be carried out on-site by architects or engineers using detailed, but not standardized, data-gathering methods. Houseowners received a report detailing the results and giving recommendations. They paid ECU75 for this advice, and an additional ECU410 was paid by the regional government. Finance of ECU1.8 million was provided for this programme, but only about ECU0.6 million has been used, which demonstrates a low level of interest by houseowners – as well as by the experts in offering these consultations. This programme was stopped when the similar federal programme (see pp. 38–9) started.

Chimney-sweeps

An initiative on the part of the chimney-sweeps' association to offer a 'weak point analysis' to private households was supported by the regional government. Chimney-sweeps are authorized by German law to control the emissions of all small and medium-size heating equipment annually. The association had worked out a standardized computer-aided method to analyse the energy quality of a building and its heating equipment and to give recommendations for energy conservation measures in the form of a written report. The regional government subsidized each consultation by paying ECU75 to the chimney-sweep in order to make it free of charge to households.

For the evaluation, questionnaires were sent to the participants of all three programmes. On average, the response was 30 per cent. The study was done by the Bremer Energie-Institut and the University of Bremen. Table 2. 2 shows the numbers of participants, questionnaires and answers and the main results of the evaluation.

Table 2.2   Methodology and main results

	Written advice	Personal audits	Chimney -sweeps
Consulted households (no.)	181	1 197	41 900
Questionnaires sent (no.)	169	835	1 200
Answers (no.)	83	227	445
Total costs of the programmes (ECU)	12 500	475 000	90 000
Costs per case (ECU)	75	560	75
Savings/public funds (kWh/ECU)	320	38	250

In summary, the written advice programmes had almost the same outcome in terms of energy conservation as the audit programmes, but expenditure of public funds was much lower so that the cost-benefit relation was much better in the written advice cases. This result supported the decision of the Hessen Government to cut the audit programme; a result that will be illustrated in a little more detail.

The respondents were asked which investments they had made as a result of the recommendations, and the cost of these investments. The energy-saving potential was calculated by the evaluators according to an existing computer program for energy conservation measures in a typical one-family house.

Table 2.3   Distribution of energy conservation investment, by type of investment and type of programme

	Written advice (%)	Personal audits (%)	Chimney-sweeps (%)
New boilers	38	40	70
Insulated windows	14	23	15
Wall insulation	29	7	3
Roof insulation	11	6	3
Others	8	24	9
Total	100	100	100

Table 2.3 shows the distribution of the money spent by the respondents on energy conservation investments for different technical measures. In all three programmes, but especially in the chimney-sweep case, the main emphasis was on the replacement of boilers. In the case of wall insulation, the highest response rate (29 per cent) was found with the written analysis programme; it is assumed that this was a consequence of the special and detailed information on this measure which was made available in the Vogelsberg region (in which this programme was tested) and the recommendation to install insulation before improving or replacing the heating equipment. The amount of wall insulation achieved by the audit programme (only 7 per cent) is regarded as insufficient. Wall insulation is the measure with the highest energy-saving potential, but it is only cost-efficient when associated with renovation of the outside walls. When walls are refurbished without insulation, the opportunity for energy conservation is forgone for many years. It is, therefore, important to give incentives in this area. With the chimney-sweep programme there is the problem that chimney-sweeps are not regarded by houseowners as experts in insulation measures.

Two-thirds of the respondents in the written advice programme and 80 per cent in the other two reacted to the recommendations and carried out at least one measure; 33 per cent of the first group, 47 per cent in the second and 58 per cent in the third were strongly persuaded by the recommendations to undertake the investment(s).

Table 2.4 Investments undertaken as a percentage of recommendations made, by type of investment

	Written analysis %	Personal advice %	Chimney-sweep %
New boilers	66	74	76
Thermostats	79	86	62
Central heating control	61	75	62
Pipe insulation	—	60	35
Hot-water system changes	—	60	49
Insulated windows	79	67	45
Wall insulation	43	17	7
Roof insulation	74	47	32
Cellar ceiling insulation	20	21	13
Insulation behind radiators	35	52	24
Electricity saving	—	79	30
Solar energy, heat pumps	—	26	9

The types of recommendations which were accepted most often differ between the three programmes. This is in part due to the fact that the degree to which measures have been dealt with, or have been discussed in detail, in the consultation varies considerably by programme. Table 2. 4 shows the investments undertaken as a percentage of recommendations made.

It should be noted that the figure of 43 per cent for acceptance of the recommendation for wall insulation (in the first programme) is high, given that such an investment is only cost-effective in association with renovation of the outside wall. Conversely, a relatively low percentage of respondents (20 per cent) followed the recommendation to insulate their cellar ceiling, which is a relatively simple and cost-efficient measure.

For the cost-benefit analysis, only those households were included who said that their investment decision was strongly influenced by the recommendations. Table 2. 5 shows the results of this analysis. Most of the energy savings were achieved by insulation measures: in the case of the written advice programme 82 per cent, the audit programme 62 per cent and the chimney-sweep programme 40 per cent of the respective totals was as a result of insulation.

Table 2.5   Cost–benefit analysis of public funds and energy savings

	Written advice	Personal audit	Chimney-sweeps
Investment decision strongly influenced (%)	33	47	58
Average investment (ECU)	6000	8000	6000
Average energy savings within 20 years (kWh)	7000	8000	4500
savings achieved (%) by:			
new boilers	10	15	34
insulation	82	62	40
heating control	8	11	23
others	-	12	3
savings/funds (kWh/ECU)	320	38	250
CO_2 reduction (kg/ECU)	80	9	60

Finally, the respondents were asked for their reasons for undertaking the investments, in order to discover the significance of the recommendations (see Table 2.6). The answer 'was planned anyway' can be regarded as a kind of 'free-rider' effect: the households have used the programme although they had already decided on an energy-saving investment. On the other hand, it seems to be important that the advice confirmed their decision.

Table 2.6   Reasons for and obstacles to investments

	Written advice %	Personal audit %	Chimney-sweeps %
Reasons for investments			
was planned anyway	61	47	25
strongly influenced by the advice	33	47	58
environment protection	31	47	36
need for renovation	25	28	12
funds were available	23	11	16
Obstacles to investments			
recommendation makes no sense	21	11	7
too expensive	17	34	27
do not believe in calculated energy savings	6	6	7
energy prices too low	5	7	3
other experts gave other advice	4	8	2
other arguments (e.g. heating system not too old)	31	37	11

Those who did not follow the recommendations were asked for their reasons. The results are relatively heterogeneous, as shown in Table 2.6. The most important reason seemed to be the high costs of the measures.

The overall result is quite clear: the 'written advice' programme was characterized by a high efficiency whereas the audit programme was rather expensive relative to the impact. The chimney-sweep programme is very interesting: this is the only group to visit all houses (and small firms) once a year and is well accepted by the houseowners as independent consultants.

OTHER EXPERIENCES

In Denmark, several programmes for private households were combined. The Heating Audit Scheme was established in 1978 in connection with a subsidy programme to promote energy savings in private households. The audit was intended to ensure proper use of the subsidies. The combination of the two measures was very successful: the number of audits peaked at 140 000 in 1984. After cutting the subsidy programme, the use of audits decreased rapidly, to about 5000 per year (1994). As an additional measure, the result of a heat inspection must be presented when selling houses or apartments. In 1978, an Oil Boiler Registration Scheme was introduced which is similar to the German Regulation: chimney-sweeps have to check the heating equipment once a year.

Both programmes were evaluated with regard to activities carried out in 1990, when there were about 5000 audits (Christensen *et al.*, 1994). Based on 227 telephone interviews with surveyed households, proposed and implemented projects and the resultant energy savings were analysed. In the case of the Registration Scheme, boilers which had been inspected were compared with those which had not.

Three years after the audit, 25 per cent of all suggestions had been carried out, 8 per cent had been partially acted upon, and 47 per cent had been rejected. Low-cost measures were most often acted upon, for example the installation of thermostatic valves or other automatic control equipment. About 80 per cent of the respondents said that they would have made the investments anyway. This is not surprising, because most people who make use of an audit are aware of energy conservation before the audit and this is the reason for seeking advice. In sum, a 1.5 per cent reduction in energy consumption was achieved taking into account the 20 per cent of households which were strongly influenced by the audit. The use of heating audit reports in connection with property sales is falling: they were presented for only 42.5 per cent of the one-family houses sold in 1992 (with some regional differences).

The evaluation of the Registration Scheme showed that about 15 per cent of boilers are not checked and registered. Half of the households surveyed in telephone interviews admitted that they had had no inspection or said that they did not know about it. The efficiency of the unregistered boilers was about 5 per cent lower compared with those which were registered.

Finally, the evaluations calculated the cost-benefit relations of the schemes. Since 1981 the heat audit has had to be fully paid for by the householders, whereas during the period 1978–81 they were subsidized by the government. The boiler inspections have to be paid for by the owners. The evaluation found that on average investments together with audit costs led to a financial loss for the households, except in the cases of very small investments and of old properties (built before 1920), where the costs and the benefit were balanced. The Registration Scheme led to a private loss per household and to a small socioeconomic loss (energy production and external costs); if carried out only every other year instead of annually, the loss would be changed into a positive balance. The authors of the evaluation study point out that it is also important to take into account the employment effects. The Registration Scheme involves cleaning, checking and adjustment. Overall, it is more labour-intensive than the Heating Audit Scheme.

CONCLUSIONS AND RECOMMENDATIONS

The suggestions of the evaluation studies described can be summarized as follows:

1. There is a need for more evaluation studies of all the types of consultation programmes and for comparisons of experiences in other countries.
2. Different target groups, for example types of houseowners, must be included in promotion programmes and be addressed specifically; for example, big companies, small owners, one-family houses, apartment owners, various social groups.
3. Environmental protection is an important value for private consumers, rated by them more highly than energy saving. Consultants should explain to their clients, therefore, the environmental benefits of energy-saving measures.
4. The chimney-sweeps are important agents, because they are the only people who visit all houses (and small firms) regularly. Their advice still concentrates on heating systems. There is a need to train them in insulation matters to improve their knowledge and acceptability as general energy consultants.
5. Consultants should use simple tools to explain the need for these measures, their cost-effectiveness and so on.
6. Local energy advice centres should be further developed in order to establish an independent source for energy consultation. All the positive elements which were identified in the evaluation studies should be combined and integrated. Written or personal recommendations should be supported by additional materials, for example informative and well-structured brochures. Such materials could be used also in the advice centres of energy utilities (which offer more and more energy consultation, concentrating on the energy supply side or the electricity sector).
7. There is still a need for more effectively promoting the insulation of existing buildings, for two reasons: to address a large energy conservation potential and to overcome the existing severe obstacles that inhibit its realization.

One last remark on methodology seems to be necessary. There exist some severe problems with regard to the evaluation of consultation programmes. First, the attribution of effects to special programmes is difficult because of multiple influencing factors, such as energy prices, information measures and others. Second, there is a response bias inherent in the fact that it is usually only interested people who are willing to answer questionnaires.

REFERENCES

Christensen, I. M. (1994), *Energikonsulenter i enfamiliehuse: En evaluering af Energiekonsulentororordningen og Oliefyrservicebranchens Registreringsordning*, Copenhagen: Arnternes og Kommunernes Forkningsinstitut rapport.

Clausnitzer, K.-D. and N. Sagehorn (1994*), Erfolgskontrolle hessischer Energieberatungsprogramme*, Bremen: Hessisches Ministerium für Umwelt, Energie und Bundesangelegenheiten.

Commission of the European Communities (1984), *Comparison of Energy Saving Programmes of EC Member States*, Brussels: Commission of the European Communities, Com (84) 36 Final.

GIS, Informationsmanagement und Systementwicklung (1990), *Vor-Ort-Beratung zur Energieeinsparung im Wohngebäudebereich*, Hamburg: Gesellschaft für antrendungsorientierte Forschung, Management- und Systemberatung.

Gruber, E. (1992), 'Efficiency of Energy Conservation Programmes in European Countries', *Energy and Environment*, **3** (2), 122–32.

Institute for Economic Research (Ifo), ISI (Fraunhofer Institut für Systemtechnik und Innovationsforschung) (1990), [Evaluation of Energy Conservation Programmes], 'Evaluierung energiepolitischer Programme zur rationellen Energienutzung', in Enquête Commission of the German Bundestag (ed.), *Energie und Klima* [Energy and Climate], vol. 10, Bonn and Karlsruhe: Economics/Müller.

Jochem, E., E. Gruber and W. Mannsbart (1996), 'German energy policy in transition', in F. McGowan (ed.), *European Energy Policies in a Changing Environment*, Heidelberg: Physica, pp. 57–87.

Karl, H.D. (1994*), Wirksamkeit von Maßnahmen zur Energiesparberatung*, Munich: Ifo-Studien zur Energiewirtschaft.

3. The case of combined heat and power in the European Union

Chris Hendriks, Jan Willem Velthuijsen, Ernst Worrell and Kornelis Blok

INTRODUCTION

Combined generation and utilization of heat and power (CHP) is a technique that reduces primary energy consumption compared to separate generation of heat and power. The savings in primary energy by small-scale CHP gas turbine units can be about 30 per cent when power generation replaces a conventional power plant and about 15 per cent when power generation replaces natural gas-fired combined cycles. The savings obtained by condensing and back-pressure steam turbines are considerably smaller. Most of the heat generated by CHP units is used for the production of steam or hot water. In the future it may also be possible to use high-temperature heat directly as process heat for industrial applications; this technique would reduce the primary energy consumption further. Generally electricity can be transported much more easily and cheaply than heat. Therefore, private producers of power must gear their CHP installation to the heat demand. In periods when less electricity is generated than is needed for own consumption, electricity must be purchased from the grid. When more electricity is generated than needed, the excess amount of electricity may be sold. An additional possibility is to make use of the grid to transport excess electricity to other users. This is called *wheeling*. In periods when the CHP unit is not in operation, all the electricity needed must be bought from the utilities; this requires back-up power. The profitability of CHP installations depends on many factors, the main ones being transition costs, investment costs, electricity price, buy-back tariffs, back-up power tariffs, fuel prices and tariffs for wheeling (when allowed).

The penetration of CHP can be accelerated by policy measures: it can be stimulated by measures that can influence the profitability of CHP installations, or it can be forced by setting standards. Stimulation of CHP involves several political problems, one of which is related to the long-term character of electricity production planning. Usually, electricity production capacity is planned on a time horizon of ten years or more, and the corresponding development decisions are taken five to ten years before the central power plant becomes operational. In contrast, decentralized power is planned on a much shorter time horizon. An increase of CHP capacity in the short term may lead to an overcapacity centrally, which could result in an increase in electricity prices if the price is based on cost recovery, where a high proportion of the costs are fixed, and if the volume of sales is decreasing.

Policy measures to stimulate the proliferation of CHP have been motivated by the energy conservation potential. In this chapter we investigate to what extent the penetration of CHP has taken place in EU-12 member states. We also analyse the potential heat demand which can be covered by CHP and the corresponding capacity for each country. A short overview is given of the CHP capacity goals for some of the EU-12 member states. We distinguish regulation, standard setting, information and economic instruments. Four different types of standard setting are given and we evaluate a specific standard setting which was applied in the Netherlands in the 1970s and early 1980s. The economic instruments are evaluated in terms of pay-back period. This pay-back period can be influenced by, for example, investment grants, taxes on the emission of carbon dioxide, increasing buy-back tariffs for electricity delivered to the public grid, or lowering the price for natural gas for CHP applications. Finally, we give some recommendations as to how EU policy could stimulate the application of CHP.

In the next section we describe the development of CHP from 1974 to 1990 in the EU-12 member states, and the stated intentions of national governments in this regard. In subsequent sections an overview is given of the potential capacity of CHP, and we discuss the instruments: standard settings and economical instruments. Finally, we provide conclusions, especially with regard to EU policy options.

THE DEVELOPMENT OF CHP CAPACITY IN THE EUROPEAN UNION

CHP-related electricity is produced by utilities (mostly in connection with district heating) and by autoproducers. In the EU-12 countries electricity production has grown from 1150 TWh in 1974 to almost 1800 TWh in 1990 (see Figure 3.1).

In the same period CHP-related electricity production by the public utilities and the autoproducers remained almost constant. The public utilities produce 32 TWh/annum and the autoproducers produce 71 TWh/annum. The share of

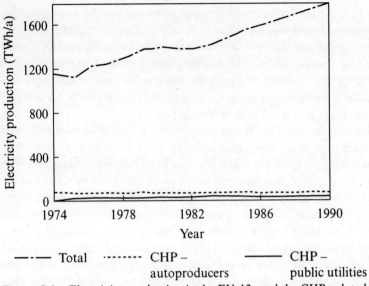

—·— Total   ······· CHP –   ——— CHP –
                      autoproducers   public utilities

Figure 3.1   Electricity production in the EU-12, and the CHP-related
              electricity production by autoproducers and the public utilities,
              1974–90

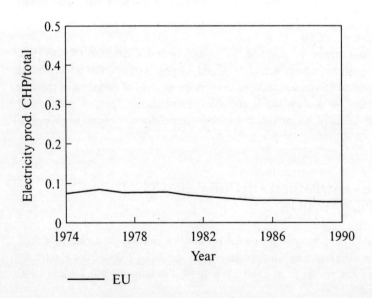

——— EU

Figure 3.2   The CHP-related electricity production by autoproducers and
              public utilities as fraction of the total electricity production in the
              EU-12, 1974–90

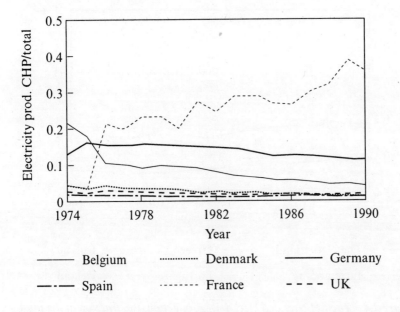

Figure 3.3   *The CHP-related electricity production as fraction of the total electricity production for Belgium, Denmark, Germany, Spain, France and the United Kingdom, 1974–90*

CHP decreased therefore from about 8 per cent in the mid-1970s to about 6 per cent in 1990 (see Figure 3.2). It should be noted that in 1988 autoproducers generated about 50 per cent of the electricity in combination with heat production. The remaining 50 per cent of the electricity is generated without simultaneous heat production (Dufait *et al.*, 1992). Data on this aspect are not available for other years.

Figures 3.3 and 3.4 show the development for the individual EU-12 countries (for method of calculation, see Box 3.1). The percentage of CHP in Belgium (B), France (F) and Germany (D) has been decreased during the period from 1974 to 1990. The percentages of CHP in Spain (E), the United Kingdom (UK), Greece (GR), Ireland (IR), Italy (I) and Portugal (P) remain more or less constant. Large growths in CHP can be found in Denmark (DK)[1] and the Netherlands (NL). It should be noted that especially for Germany, France, Italy and the United Kingdom the amount of electricity produced by autoproducers without heat production is relatively high compared to the other EU-12 members.

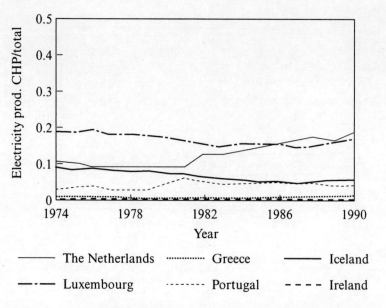

Figure 3.4   *The CHP-related electricity production as a fraction of the total*
electricity production for the Netherlands, Greece, Italy,
Luxembourg, Portugal, and Ireland, 1974–90

Table 3.1   *Installed CHP-related electricity generating capacity, 1989*

Country	Industrial CHP installed capacity (MW$_e$)
Belgium	340
Denmark	140
Germany	8 450
Greece	40
Spain	962
France	1 980
Ireland	58
Italy	4 630
Luxembourg	–
Netherlands	1 820
Portugal	388
United Kingdom	1 793
Total	2 0601

Source: Dufait *et al.* (1992).

Box 3.1

Method of calculation of CHP-related electricity production in the EU-12

The basis of the calculation is the data for a period of 17 years (1974–90) provided by the annual reports of the International Energy Agency (IEA) statistics entitled *Energy Balances of OECD countries* (IEA, 1960–90). The total electricity production of each country for each year is calculated as the sum of the fields 'Public electricity + CHP' and 'Autoproducers of Electricity'. The CHP-related electricity production is calculated as the sum of CHP-related electricity production by public utilities and the autoproducers. The contribution of the public utilities is calculated based on the assumption that electricity and heat in a CHP unit (generally these are conventional steam-electric power plants) are produced in a ratio of 0.3 to 0.5. At periods in which less heat is produced and more electricity, not all the electricity is regarded as CHP-related produced electricity. Hence, our figures differ from those given in the IEA statistics.

The CHP-related electricity production by autoproducers is the total amount of produced electricity by autoproducers minus electricity produced by 'Hydro', 'Geothermal, solar etc.' and 'Nuclear'. Furthermore, a correction is made for the electricity produced without heat production. The ratio of electricity production with and without simultaneous heat production varies from country to country. As far as we know, this ratio is only given for the year 1988 by Dufait *et al.* (1992). It is assumed that, during the years considered, this ratio has been constant.

Another unit in which to express the role of CHP in electricity production is the share of installed capacity. The percentage of installed capacity will not necessarily be equal to the percentage of produced electricity. The load of the CHP units depends on many factors, such as the type of industrial use, but also on the buy-back tariffs for the generated electricity supplied to the grid. Based on national statistics, and thus inevitably based on different nomenclatures, the installed capacity in the EU-12 in 1989 is determined (Dufait *et al.*, 1992) (see Table 3.1). The installed capacity in the EU-12 amounts to 20 600 Mega Watt equivalent (MW_e), which represents about 8 per cent of the total installed capacity in the EU-12. The CHP-related produced electricity accounts for 6 per cent of the total generated electricity. From these figures it can be concluded that the load factor of the CHP capacity on average is lower than the load factor of non-CHP capacity.

For the period after 1990 limited data are available. An overview of (projected) CHP capacities for some EU-12 countries is given below (Brown, 1994; De Vos, 1994; IEA, 1994). In Belgium, in the national programme for reducing greenhouse emissions, the forecast is that 500 MW$_e$ of CHP in the industrial sector can be installed by the year 2000. In the tertiary sector a potential of 200 MW$_e$ is foreseen. In Denmark the Energy 2000 programme (DME, 1990) is expected to result in a capacity level of about 1200 MW$_e$ from decentralized small-scale CHP plants for district heating. In addition, some 300 MW$_e$ of industrial CHP is expected in addition to the 120 MW$_e$ already in place. In France since the early 1990s CHP has grown slowly by about 50 MW$_e$ per year, mainly in the tertiary sector (IEA, 1994). As part of a wider framework announced by the government of Ireland, it is expected that an additional 20 MW$_e$ of CHP capacity will be installed before 1997 (ibid.). CHP produced nearly 9 per cent of total electricity production in Italy in 1992 (ibid.). In Luxembourg research indicates that there is room for about 50 MW$_e$ of CHP (ibid.). In the Netherlands installed capacity increased from about 2250 MW$_e$ in 1990 (excluding district heating) to about 4000 MW$_e$ in 1993. By the year 2000 an extra 6000 MW$_e$ is projected to be installed by the energy companies of which about 1000 MW$_e$ (excluding district heating) is planned by the electricity production companies, and 4000 MW$_e$ is planned by the energy distribution companies (excluding district heating). The distribution and production companies also announced plans for the installation of district heating with a total capacity of about 1150 Mw$_e$.

In Spain the National Energy Plan projects an increase of more than 1250 MW$_e$ CHP capacity of autoproducers in the year 2000 compared to 1990, which means more than doubling the 1990 capacity of 950 MW$_e$ (IEA, 1994). In the United Kingdom the 1990 installed capacity amounted to about 2000 MW$_e$ (3 per cent of UK capacity). It is expected that this amount will be doubled by the year 2000, the largest part coming from medium to large installations in the industrial sector. The government target is to reach an installed capacity of 5000 MW$_e$. In 1994 the installed capacity was 3000 MW$_e$.

POTENTIALS FOR CHP IN THE EUROPEAN UNION

Improvement in the efficient use of energy is generally considered as a main option to reduce the growth of energy use and hence reduce the growth of the CO_2 emissions. One option for improving efficient energy use is to combine the production of heat and power (CHP). In some cases, the efficient use of energy of an existing CHP unit based on a boiler can be improved by replacing it by a CHP unit based on a gas turbine.

Potentials

To get an idea of the potential amount of energy that can be saved by CHP, the boundaries are set by maximum potential (upper) and the amount of energy that will be saved automatically (lower). The room for extra saving can be found between these two potentials. The potential which will most probably be reached is the one which is profitable.

The maximum potential can be calculated by assuming that the total heat demand (steam and hot water) in the industry and a (realistic) part of the heat demand in other sectors is covered by CHP units.[2] This potential is called the (reasonable) maximum potential; it is shown in Table 3.3 for each of the EU-12 countries in 1990. An explanation of the calculation method is given in Box 3.2. This potential will not be completely reached because of economic, political or logistic barriers, and because of competition from other technologies that might be equally energy efficient, for example, heat pumps.

Table 3.2   Fraction fuel used for steam and hot water production in the industrial sector in the Netherlands which can be covered by CHP

Industry	Coverage by CHP (%)
Iron and steel	10
Chemical and petrochemical	19
Non-ferrous metals	20
Non-metallic minerals	2
Transport equipment	2
Machinery	similar to Transport Equipment
Mining and quarrying	—
Food and tobacco	61
Paper, pulp and printing	91
Wood and wood products	—
Construction	similar to Non-metallic minerals
Textile and leather	12
Non-specified	—
Total	24

Sources: The data for fuel use is taken from IEA (1960–90). The heat demand is derived from data in De Beer *et al.* (1994), Wijk *et al.* (1992) and Blok and Worrell (1992).

Box 3.2
Reasonable maximum potential

To determine the potential of CHP in the EU it is necessary to know how much heat and electricity is already produced by CHP units and how much is the (reasonable) maximum potential. To calculate the (reasonable) maximum potential for the individual EU countries and the EU as a whole the following method is used.

The sectors in which CHP can be applied on large scale are identified. These sectors are Industry, Commerce and service and Residential. The sector Industry is classified into industrial activities. The classification has been taken from the IEA (IEA, 1960–90). For industrial activities, the heat demand for process heat and the heat demand for steam/hot water is determined. It is assumed that only the heat demand for steam/hot water can be covered by CHP units. As a benchmark the Dutch fuel use for heat production compared to the total fuel use is taken. It is assumed that the fraction of fuel use for the production of steam/hot water will be the same for all EU-12 countries. The ratio of the heat demand in each Dutch industrial activity is therefore used for all EU countries. Table 3.2 shows the fraction of the heat demand for steam/hot water and fuel use for each industrial activity.

The heat demand for the Commerce and Service sector is determined by taking the expected fraction of heat demand relevant to CHP determined for the Netherlands in the year 2015. This percentage is applied to each EU country unless specific data for the country were available. Detailed information on the method of determination of the percentage coverage of the Commerce and service sector can be found in De Beer *et al.* (1994). For Residential, the same calculation method as for Commerce and service is used. The coverage for the Netherlands will be 50 per cent in the year 2015 (ibid.). This percentage is applied to all EU-12 countries, except for the southern countries (Portugal, Spain, Italy and Greece) and Ireland, which have very low population densities.

The CHP-related heat demand is converted to electricity from CHP units. The calculation is done by assuming that a CHP unit produces 0.5 units of heat and 0.3 units electricity for each unit of fuel. Table 3.3 shows the percentage coverage of CHP-related electricity production in relation to the total electricity production for the year 1990. This percentage would be higher where the CHP unit does not run on full heat capacity and the load of the CHP unit is shifted to electricity production.

The heat demand is taken from Van Wijk *et al.* (1992) and the BIN database (Blok and Worrell, 1992).

Instruments

The profitable potential is the amount of CHP that will be installed when economic criteria are satisfied. These criteria are set by the institution(s) which finance(s) the programme. Profitable potentials can be estimated with reliability only when much is known about the industry. An overview of economic potentials has been made, as far as we know, only for the Netherlands (Blok and Turkenburg, 1994).

Without regulations set by the government, the realized CHP capacity may at best be equal to the profitable potential. There are several types of measure that can be applied which may increase the profitable amount of CHP. In the next section, we distinguish two types: standards setting and economic measures. These measures can be applied to cover the difference between the (reasonable) maximum potential for CHP and the present amount of CHP-generated electricity.

Table 3.3 *Amount of CHP-related electricity production in each of the EU-12 countries and the (reasonable) maximum electricity production potential by CHP*

	CHP (1990)[a] (TWh)	Total potential[b] (TWh)	Fraction of 1990 production covered[c](%)	Industry[d] (%)	Commerce and Service[e] (%)	Residential[f] (%)
Belgium	3	43	62	16	13	33
Denmark	9	11	42	13	4	25
Germany	51	245	55	14	15	26
Spain	2	42	28	14	4	11
France	6	165	40	10	21	8
UK	6	170	54	13	9	32
Netherlands	12	54	75	35	<— 40 —>	
Greece	0	9	26	9	2	15
Ireland	0	9	61	18	14	30
Italy	11	128	60	17	2	42
Luxembourg	0	3	416	146	94	176
Portugal	1	8	30	19	3	8
Total	101	886				

Notes:
[a] Amount of CHP-related electricity production in each of the EU-12 countries.
[b] The (reasonable) maximum electricity production potential by CHP.
[c] The total fraction of 1990 electricity production that could be covered by CHP if the (reasonable) maximum potential were realized.
[d] Sector as function of 1990 electricity production.
[e] The sectoral percentages for Spain, France, Ireland and Italy do not add up due to rounding.
[f] For the Netherlands, the 40% is for Common Service and Residential combined.

REGULATION INSTRUMENTS IN THE EUROPEAN UNION MEMBER STATES

The position of CHP differs strongly among the EU-member states. Figures 3.3 and 3.4 clearly show a stable increase of CHP-based electricity production in the Netherlands and Denmark. In this section we analyse the (political) factors in this development. Because the implementation of CHP has been successful in these two countries, we restrict our analysis to them. Later we give a more general description of economic instruments which may stimulate the application of CHP.

The Netherlands

A detailed description of the development of installed CHP capacity and CHP-related electricity production in the Netherlands is given by Blok (1993) and Blok and Farla (1996). Two main actors in the development of CHP in the years 1988–93 can be distinguished: the national government and the energy utilities.

Up to 1978 not much attention was paid to CHP in government energy reports, but from then on the government introduced various CHP-stimulating measures and played a major role in the negotiation and implementation of agreements between utilities and industry. In 1987 government policy was set out in the Stimulation Programme on CHP. In this programme a continuation of investment grants for CHP and the establishment of a CHP bureau (Projectbureau Warmte/Kracht – PW/K) was announced. This bureau was to function as a broker for the achievement of CHP projects. The government provided funds for research and development programmes addressed to energy-saving instruments and also gave grants up to 25 per cent of total investment costs for demonstration plants; occasionally the grant was raised to 40 per cent. The government also initiated subsidies of up to 50 per cent of the costs of CHP feasibility studies. In 1993 the official target for CHP capacity was set at 8000 MW_e by the year 2000. At the same time a reduction in subsidies was announced, because they no longer appeared necessary for further development of large-scale CHP installations.

The main policy instrument with respect to CHP during this period was the investment subsidy for CHP, although its contribution to total investment has been fairly modest, at about 10 per cent (Blok and Farla, 1996). In the same period the energy companies started environmental action plans. In 1990 the energy distribution companies announced a goal of more than 2000 MW_e of CHP to be installed in the year 2000. In 1994, the plan was updated to 4000 MW_e, excluding district heating. The electricity production companies planned about

1000 MW$_e$. The distribution and production companies also announced plans for the installation of district heating with a total capacity of about 1150 MW$_e$.

The actual realization of installed capacity in the period from 1990 to 1993 amounted to 270 MW$_e$ per year. The concrete investment plans put forward in the same period (in the form of a subsidy request) amounted to 900 MW$_e$ per year on average.

The energy companies stimulated the installation of CHP in the following ways:

- investing in CHP installation completely at their own risk;
- forming a joint venture with an industrial company. The legal construction of the joint venture is such that 'off balance sheet' financing is possible. In this way the internal rate of return (IRR) can be higher than in the case of own investment and the pay-back time can be reduced by a factor of 3 (PW/K, 1992).

Measures to stimulate CHP have been taken in the Netherlands since 1978. We can conclude that since then the installed CHP capacity has increased substantially. The question can be posed whether the measures to stimulate installation caused the increase of CHP capacity or whether it would have been increased without them. According to Blok and Turkenburg (1994), the CHP capacity that would have been implemented in the manufacturing industry would have amounted to only a few hundred MW$_e$, and this would have been mirrored in other sectors. Therefore, we conclude that without stimulation not much CHP capacity would have been realized.

The main criterion for investment in CHP capacity is the payback period of the installation. Blok and Turkenburg (1994) state that feasible CHP capacity is negligible when the criterion of a three-year simple payback period must be satisfied. The realizable CHP capacity goes up almost proportionally to 1300 MW$_e$ for a simple payback period of seven years. Industrial companies generally accept projects with payback periods of from one to seven years, with an average of four years (Gruber and Brand, 1991; Koot *et al.*, 1984; Velthuijsen, 1995). This holds for energy-efficient equipment as well as for core business equipment. When we consider that the investment grant is 25 per cent, it can be calculated that this reduces the payback period by one-quarter. The payback period is heavily influenced by the activities of the energy companies: this is confirmed by the list of investors for large projects in 1993. About three-quarters of the total capacity was placed by or in co-operation with the energy companies. It should be noted that in the same period covenants were made with the government which could have affected willingness to invest in CHP.

Denmark

In Denmark almost 50 per cent of the non-industrial heat market in 1990 was covered by district heating (DH); this is a much larger share than in other EU-12 countries (Nielsen, 1994). This large CHP/DH share is the consequence of actions taken after the first oil crisis. At that time Denmark was very vulnerable in terms of oil supply. After the oil crisis it was decided to switch from oil to coal in power plants. Nowadays, CHP plans are a result of the target to reduce CO_2- emissions from the energy sector by 20 per cent by 2005 compared to 1988 (Pedersen, 1994; Pedersen and Staerkind, n.d.). In 1979, the parliament decided to allocate natural gas from Danish gas fields for industrial and space heating use. This project has been one of the key factors in the implementation of CHP in Denmark. Furthermore, a Heat Supply Act was enacted to encourage the introduction of natural gas and CHP in power plants to serve the space heating market. The Heat Supply Acts initiated a planning process involving local, regional and national authorities, utilities and fuel suppliers. After 1986, smaller cities were assumed to be connected to DH networks. In this programme, the power companies played a leading role as contractors and owners of CHP plants. No legislation was enacted to support this agreement. In 1990, in the revised Heat Supply Act, it was decided that new electricity capacity must be based on small-scale CHP plants fuelled by natural gas, refuse or biomass. Furthermore, the Act placed an obligation on all municipalities to ensure that the local heat markets are available for potential CHP plant operators.

The projects were driven partly by mandatory measures and partly by price policies and by setting taxes and subsidies. Examples of mandatory measures include: (a) the Heat Supply Act, enabling the Minister of Energy to issue general or site-specific guidelines for CHP planning, and (b) giving municipalities a right to impose compulsory connection of consumers to the district heating network. Price agreements are: (a) a buy-back tariff based on the avoided costs of a coal-fired power plant with SO_x and NO_x abatement equipment and avoided distribution costs; (b) grid connection costs paid by an independent power producer; (c) about 50 per cent of the natural gas bought for half the price that would be paid for heating-only boilers. Furthermore, grants are available for new DH networks (40 per cent of investment) and renovation projects (20 per cent). From 1986, the independent power producers were given the option of indexed loans. The interest rate is low and the repayment schedule is adjusted for inflation.

Conclusion

In two of the twelve EU member states the installed CHP capacity has substantially increased during the last decade. In the Netherlands this has been achieved mainly by industrial autoproducers, and in Denmark mainly by district heating. It has been shown for the Netherlands that the capacity that would be installed autonomously is much smaller than what has actually been installed. The energy companies are the main actors in achieving the large increase in installed capacity; they supported industrial companies with financial facilities and with information. From 1990 covenants and environment licences may also have played a role in the stimulation of CHP. We were not able to determine the effect of covenants, although it should be noted that the activity of the energy distribution companies was also initiated by an agreement with the Dutch government. In Denmark standard setting as well as price policies, taxes and subsidies are used to stimulate CHP, especially via district heating. We could not determine how large the influences were of each regulation instrument.

Standard Setting and Regulation

In environmental policy, standards have been often applied (Opschoor *et al.*, 1994). However, in energy policy standard setting is only applied in a few cases. In many countries energy efficiency standards are used for the thermal performance of new buildings (Janda and Busch, 1994), and to a smaller extent, for cars and electric appliances (IEA, various years). For other sectors, such as the manufacturing industry and also the power conversion industry, energy efficiency standards are rare. An example of the regulatory approach to energy conversion efficiency was the regulation in the Netherlands which did not permit the use of more than 10 million m^3 natural gas in steam boilers (later this figure was changed to 30 million m^3) (Blok, 1993). This restriction was abolished in 1983. We next discuss the restrictions on the application of standard setting and evaluate the effect on energy savings of such standards.

Preconditions for the effective application of standard setting and regulation

The application of standard setting must be judged against other kinds of instrument. Instruments can be evaluated on the basis of various criteria, such as effectiveness, efficiency and unwanted side-effects. An instrument is effective when the specified objective is reached. Mandatory regulations can be very effective; for example, if boilers are prohibited, industry must switch to more energy-efficient gas turbines. In the case of financial instruments, it is always uncertain how the market will react.

An instrument is efficient if the instrument can be applied with a minimum of both effort and means. Mandatory regulations are often inefficient for several reasons: they involve a lot of administrative work; often prohibitions have to be monitored and this requires inspectors; when the rule is violated the violator must be prosecuted and this requires legal evidence. All this can make regulation an expensive instrument. Unwanted side-effects may be that implementation of the measure may be disproportionately expensive for individual companies, and industries of individual countries may face a competitive disadvantage compared to the industries in countries which do not apply that regulation. Finally, a policy measure should not impose a disproportionate cost on industry. For example, if a company uses steam only a few hours per year, it should be excluded from this measure. This potential problem may be avoided by excluding companies which can show that the measure exceeds a stated percentage of the internal rate of return (IRR) on investment, but the assessment of such claims also imposes administrative burdens.

The costs for the companies may be decreased by forming a joint venture with non-industrial partners, such as the utilities and the service companies. Additional conditions for the introduction of a measure are that the local (responsible) authorities must be properly informed, the measure must be capable of being monitored, and the measure must not prohibit or counteract innovative technologies.

Types and examples of regulation
Standards for CHP can take various forms. Four general forms are discussed here and examples given.

Prohibition measure   Under such a measure a specified technology may not be used. An example is the law prohibiting steam generation in boilers that use more than a certain amount of fuel. In the Netherlands, such a ban has a precedent: in the 1970s, it was no longer permitted to use more than 10 million m of natural gas per year (later this figure was increased to 30 million m) for steam generation in a boiler. The purpose of this ban was to preserve Dutch natural gas reserves. The restriction was abolished at the beginning of the 1980s because the government stated that price would be the main determining factor for the allocation of natural gas.

Mandatory requirement   For certain purposes a particular technology must be used. An example is the law in Denmark that, under certain conditions, newly built houses must be equipped with district heating.

Covenant   An agreement between (associations of) industrial companies and the government. At present such covenants are the main pillar of the government's industrial energy conservation policy in the Netherlands. In general, the agreement is to reduce the energy consumption per unit of product by a certain percentage. CHP is one of the techniques that can be used to reach this goal.

Environmental licence   This involves setting environmental standards for certain industrial activities. An example is the law that energy must be used in such a way that conversion efficiency does not fall below a certain limit. A requirement for an environmental licence may be an obligation to utilize the best available technology that does not entail excessive costs.

Influence of regulations on energy savings and CO2 emissions

For the Netherlands, the effect of a covenant has been calculated on the basis of penetration of CHP capacity satisfying a preset value of the internal rate of return (IRR) and the effect of forbidding the burning of fuel in conventional boilers above a preset maximum (Blok and Turkenburg, 1994). For the latter, it was shown that if the restriction were set at 30 million m^3 natural gas equivalent of fuel, about 1600 MW_e of CHP capacity would have been installed, divided over 23 plants. This capacity is equivalent to 9 per cent of total Dutch power capacity. If the restriction were set at 5 million m^3 of natural gas equivalent the capacity which would be installed amounts to 2400 MW_e, that is, 14 per cent of total Dutch installed capacity. The reduction in CO_2 emission amounts to 4.7 and 6.5 Mtonnes respectively for the restriction of 30 million m^3 and of 5 million m^3, respectively. These values represent 9 per cent and 13 per cent respectively of total Dutch CO_2 emission by industrial activities.

Table 3.4   The effect of legislation on installed CHP capacity and CO_2 emissions avoided

	CHP capacity (MW$_e$)	Number of plants	Avoided CO$_2$ emission (ktonne)[a]
Restrictons on fuel[b]			
max. 5 Mm (Million M³/AN)	2400	123	6520 (13%)
max. 10 Mm	2080	69	5880 (11%)
max. 30 Mm	1590	23	4650 (9%)
Covenants[c]			
IRR = 10%	1770	62	5300 (10%)
IRR = 15%	1200	23	3830 (8%)

Notes:
[a]   Figure in brackets represents the percentage of CO_2 avoided out of the total industrial CO_2 emitted.
[b]   Forbids the burning of fuel in conventional boilers over a preset annual maximum.
[c]   All CHP investments must satisfy a preset internal rate of return (IRR).

Source: Blok and Turkenburg (1994).

Another possible way to mandate the application of CHP is to set criteria on the basis of the IRR. This can be achieved by legislation, for example, as a part

of the environmental licence, but also by means of a covenant which specifies
that all investment opportunities which meet a pre-set internal rate of return (IRR)
will be undertaken. Setting financial criteria gives better assurance that a given
target will be achieved at the lowest possible costs. To be effective this IRR
criterion should be lower than that normally required for industrial investments.
An IRR threshold value of 10 per cent or 15 per cent corresponding to a
simple payback period of 9 and 6.5 years, respectively, could result in the
realization of installed industrial CHP capacity in the Netherlands of 1770 and
1200 MW$_e$, respectively. The avoided CO_2 emissions would then amount to 5.3
and 3.8 Mtonnes, corresponding to 11 per cent and 8 per cent reductions in
industrial CO_2 emissions respectively. An overview of the effects of these criteria
is given in Table 3.4.

Economic Instruments

Historically, electricity production and distribution has been a public service
strongly influenced by governments. All investments have been carefully
considered and decisions have involved economic and political arguments.
This was in the context of a monopolistic electricity sector. Nowadays we witness
tendencies in Europe towards bringing market influences to bear on the energy
sector, and in particular towards greater liberalization of the energy markets.

Pricing policy

In theory, the installation of a CHP unit becomes attractive as soon as the
payback period becomes 'short enough' or the internal rate of return 'high
enough'. In practice, there are several obstacles which influence the decision
of the business: lack of information, problems of access to financial sources and,
most importantly, energy prices which are too low to justify concerns about
efficiency improvements and the corresponding cost savings in the first place
(Velthuijsen, 1995).

Essentially there are four mechanisms for stimulating the installation of
CHP via economic instruments:

- by stimulating the purchase of the installation via subsidies or tax
  deductions;
- by stimulating energy conservation by energy taxes or carbon taxes;
- by enabling sell-back and 'wheeling' and by setting an attractive tariff;
- by stimulating the involvement of energy companies (for example,
  encouraging energy companies to undertake joint ventures with industrial
  companies, or to handle the total investment in the CHP installation).

The first type of instrument is well documented, both theoretically and with respect to their practical effectiveness (Blok, 1993; Blok and Turkenburg, 1994; Blok and Farla, 1996; WRR, 1992). Subsidies and tax deduction facilities increase the IRR and shorten the payback period. The costs of compliance are generally lower than for regulation measures, although the costs of the fiscal institutions that govern the subsidies and the tax forms are not negligible. The third type of instrument – sell-back and wheeling at an attractive tariff – is not yet documented at length, as far as we know, as it is fairly specific to the technology (together with electricity produced from other autoproducing installations, such as solar power, wind power, biomass and waste-burning power).

Table 3.5   Official regulation of grid connection conditions

	Technical prescriptions	Tariffs
Belgium	partly	<15 kV grid
Denmark	no	yes
Germany	no	partly
Greece	yes	yes
Spain	yes	yes
France	yes	yes
Italy	> 3 MW$_e$	yes
Luxembourg	—	yes
Netherlands	yes	yes
Portugal	yes	yes
United Kingdom	yes	purchase < 1 MW$_e$

Source: Dufait (1993).

As Table 3.5 indicates, the supply of excess CHP-produced electricity to the grid is regulated in some form virtually everywhere throughout the EU, but regulations differ across member states. In most countries there are technical prescriptions: Denmark and Germany are the notable exceptions. With respect to tariffs for autoproducers, conditions also vary across member states (see Table 3.5). Except in Belgium (for large firms), Germany and Greece, it seems that co-generators are not discriminated against *vis-à-vis* other electricity suppliers in respect of complementary electricity deliveries. Co-generators cannot subscribe to a user-driven separate contract for back-up power in Belgium, Denmark, Spain, France and Portugal. In a few countries – Germany, Greece, France and the UK – utilities refuse to accept deliveries of co-generated electricity where there is restricted grid capacity.

An overview of 1993 buy-back tariffs in the EU member states is given in Novem (1994). In this study the tariffs are evaluated in two ways: first, in terms of the official absolute price per kWh, and second, in relative terms, that is, relative to the integral fixed and variable costs of capacity and electricity *purchased*. As there are different tariffs for different amounts purchased at different periods in time, the tariffs are compared for five selected types of CHP installations, which vary with respect to capacity and number of hours per year. These latter tariffs dictate to what extent selling and buying is competitive, and to what extent the selling back of excess electricity is an economically important consideration when considering installation of CHP. Table 3.6 shows some characteristics of the tariffs.

Table 3.6   Tariff conditions for independent co-generators

	Complementary electricity: co-generators distinguished from other suppliers?	Back-up power: choice of user-driven separate contracts?	Deliveries to grid: capacity allowance?
Belgium	yes, large firms	no	yes
Denmark	no	no	yes
Germany	yes/no	yes	yes/no
Greece	no	yes	no
Spain	no	no	yes
France	no	no	for guaranteed deliveries
Italy	no	yes	yes
Luxembourg	no	yes	yes
Netherlands	no	yes	yes
Portugal	no	no	yes
United Kingdom	no	yes/no	yes/no

The tariffs vary significantly across member states. Furthermore, if the rates are evaluated relative to the integral cost price of purchased electricity, both the *level* of return on sold electricity and the *spread* for different capacities and operation times differ significantly. Apparently, supplying electricity to the grid is more economical in one country than in another, and for one type of capacity and operation period than for another.

In the early 1990s, the average EU level of the absolute selling-back tariff was 0.04 ECU/kWh. Italy had the highest general absolute tariffs at 0.07 ECU/kWh, followed at a distance by Denmark and Germany: 0.05 ECU/kWh. The UK had the lowest tariffs: 0.03 ECU/kWh (see Table 3.7). The tariffs decline

Table 3.7   Selling back tariffs for electricity produced by renewable energy carriers (in ECU/kWh)

	Biomass	CHP absolute	CHP relative[a]	Hydro	Waste	Wind
Belgium	3.3	3.3	20–85	3.7	3.3	2.8
Denmark	7.9	4.7	90	4.7	5.6	5.1
France	3.7	3.3	75–95	4.7	3.7	4.2
Germany	7.0	4.7	50–100	7.0	4.7	8.4
Italy	13.0	6.5	30–130	7.0	13.0	6.5
Netherlands	3.7	3.7	75–95	3.7	3.7	3.3
United Kingdom	7.4	2.8	40–100	7.9	8.4	14.9

Note: [a] Ratio between remuneration of co-generation electricity (energy + capacity) supplied to the grid and the price of electricity purchased from the grid at the same voltage level.

Sources: Novem (1994); Dufait (1993).

Table 3.8   Possibility of wheeling and official regulation of wheeling charges

	Wheeling allowed?	Wheeling charges officially regulated?
Belgium	yes/no	no
Denmark	no	—
Germany	rarely	no
Greece	no	—
Spain	no	—
France	to affiliates	yes
Italy	to affiliates	yes
Luxembourg	no	—
Netherlands	if co-generator is large consumer	yes
Portugal	by law, not yet regulated	—
United Kingdom	third party, > 1 MW_e	yes

Source: Dufait (1993).

with increasing operation time, except in Germany (because of the so-called availability premiums). In relative terms, the tariff was highest in Denmark for units operating less than 4000 hours: 80 per cent of the final use tariffs (FUT). For longer time operational units and for larger capacity units, the Italian rates were highest. The UK and Belgium had the lowest relative rates. In Belgium and the Netherlands the tariffs for CHP electricity did not differ from the rates for electricity produced by biomass, wind, hydro and waste burning. In the other countries, however, the CHP rate seems to be among the lowest, indicating an implicit subsidy on the use of renewable sources.

Finally, the possibility of wheeling, that is, selling excess electricity directly to another user via the public grid, is allowed in Belgium, Germany, France, Italy, the Netherlands and the UK, but only under certain restrictive conditions (see Table 3.8). Except in Belgium and Germany, charges are regulated officially.

CONCLUSIONS AND EU POLICY RECOMMENDATIONS

The share of CHP-related electricity production in the EU-12 decreased during the period 1974–90. Exceptions to this trend are Denmark and the Netherlands. The present average share in the EU-12 is estimated to be 6 per cent.

For the stimulation of CHP two types of measure can be distinguished: regulations or standard setting (prohibition, enforcement, covenants and environmental licences) and economic instruments. It has been shown for the Netherlands that the actually installed amount of capacity is higher than that which would have been installed autonomously. The main actors for the large increase in installed capacity are the energy companies, which invest in CHP at their own risk. In Denmark, there is also important involvement of the energy companies. Besides financial instruments, a number of regulations are used to stimulate CHP (especially district heating).

If the need for further penetration of CHP installations in the EU is acknowledged, for instance, for reasons of economizing on energy use or reducing CO_2 emissions, the EU policy should focus on the following measures:

- harmonizing tariff structures for CHP;
- non-discrimination against companies with CHP installation which purchase complementary electricity, in terms of tariffs *vis-à-vis* other companies;
- basing tariffs for back-up power (installed power by energy companies which can be used in case of the breakdown of the CHP unit) on real costs;
- basing buy-back tariffs for electricity on the basis of long-term avoided costs, that is, including savings on power costs and fuel costs and in some cases savings on distribution costs and environmental levies also;
- the use of grid (wheeling) on a real-cost base;
- the incorporation of active participation by the energy companies, for example as in Denmark and the Netherlands. This can be done by starting with concrete environmental goals and participating in investment

structures. The financial involvement can take the form of a joint venture or the utility can conduct the investment at its own risk;

- removing the high starting costs for CHP equipment by the provision of subsidies and tax deductions. It should also be noted that investment in CHP equipment which would have been made anyway may be subsidized (free-rider effect), but some free-riding can be avoided by screening projects.

NOTES

1. For Denmark the amount of CHP-related produced electricity by the public utilities is probably somewhat overestimated, because some publicly produced heat is not related to electricity production but produced in supplementary boilers.
2. In principle process heat can also be supplied by 'high-temperature CHP' units. In that case the exhaust heat of gas turbines is led directly or indirectly (via a waste heat oil heater) to the furnace. However, this requires the complete replacement of the existing furnace because the radiative heat transfer from the gas turbine exhaust is much smaller than from combustion gases, due to their lower temperature (Blok and Turkenburg, 1994).

REFERENCES

Blok, K. (1993), 'The development of industrial CHP in the Netherlands', *Energy Policy*, **21**, 158–75.

Blok, K. and J. Farla (1996), 'The continuing story of CHP in the Netherlands', *International Journal of Global Energy Issues*, **8**, 349–61.

Blok, K. and W.C. Turkenburg (1994), 'CO_2 emission reduction by means of industrial CHP in the Netherlands', *Energy Conservation Management*, **35**, 317–40.

Blok, K. and E. Worrell (1992), 'Heat and electricity consumption of large industrial energy users in the Netherlands', *Heat Recovery Systems & CHP*, **12**, 407–17.

Brown, M. (1994), 'Combined heat and power: positive progress in the UK', *Energy Policy*, **22**, 173–7.

Danish Ministry of Energy (DME) (1990), *Energy 2000: A Plan of Action for Sustainable Development*, Copenhagen: DME.

De Beer, J.G., M.T. Wees, E. Worrell and K. Blok (1994), *ICARUS-3: The Potential of Energy Efficiency Improvement in the Netherlands up to 2000 and 2015*, Utrecht: Department of Science, Technology and Society.

De Vos, R.C.J. (1994), 'Warmte/Kracht in Europa', *Energie en Milieuspectrum*, No.11, 14–17.

Dufait, N. (1993), 'Attitudes of the electric utilities towards CHP in the EC-member states', paper presented at the European Workshop on CHP, Lisbon, Portugal, 14 December.

Dufait, N., A. Martens, J.F. Guilmot and A. Verbruggen (1992), *Industrial Cogeneration in Europe*, Mol, Belgium: VITO.

Gruber, E. and M. Brand (1991), 'Promoting energy conservation in small and medium-sized companies', *Energy Policy*, **19**, 279–87.

International Energy Agency (IEA) (1960–90), *Energy Balances of OECD Countries*, Paris: OECD/IEA.

70 A guide to policies for energy conservation

International Energy Agency (IEA) (1994), *Combined Heat and Power Generation in IEA Member Countries*, Paris: International Energy Agency.

International Energy Agency (IEA). *Energy Policies of IEA Countries*, Paris: International Energy Agency.

Janda, K.B. and J.F. Busch (1994), 'Worldwide status of energy standard for buildings', *Energy*, **19**, 27–44.

Koot, L.W., M.H. Brascamp, G. Gerritse, G.J.A.M. Meijer, A.G. Melman, and H.J. Munter (1984), *Evaluatie van de Werking en Effectiviteit van de Energietoeslag op de WIR-basispremie* [Evaluation of the Operation and Effectiveness of the Energy Bonus Added to the Base Grant of the Investment Account Act], Apeldoorn, Netherlands: Netherlands Organization for Applied Scientific Research TNO.

Nielsen, F.G. (1994), 'CHP in Denmark', paper presented at the European Workshop on CHP and Cogeneration, Soerop Manor, Ringsted, Denmark.

Novem (1994), 'Internationale Tariefsvergelijking Teruggeleverde Electriciteit' (International Comparison of Buyback Tariffs of Electricity), Report no. 9403, Hilversum, Netherlands: ERBEKO Raadgevende Ingenieurs.

Opschoor, J.B., J.B. Vos, and A.F. De Savornin Lohman (1994), *Managing the Environment: The Use of Economic Instruments*, Paris: OECD.

Pedersen, S.L. (1994), 'Examples of governmental policies to promote gas-fired cogeneration', paper presented to the IEA Workshop on Gas-fired Electric Power Generating Technologies, Madrid, Spain.

Pedersen, S.L. and K. Staerkind (n.d.), *Large Scale Deployment of Cogeneration in the Danish Energy System: Regulatory, Institutional, Economical and Technical Aspects*, Copenhagen: Danish Energy Agency.

Projektbureau Warmte/Kracht (PW/K) (1992), *Operating a Cogeneration Plant in a Joint Venture, Part Two*, Driebergen-Rijsenburg, Netherlands: Projektbureau Warmte/Kracht.

Velthuijsen, J.W. (1995), *Determinants of Investment in Energy Efficiency*, PhD. thesis, University of Groningen, The Netherlands.

Wijk, A.J.M. van, W. Gilijamse and E. Worrell (1992), *Analyse van Warmtevoorziening: Programmastudie voor het SYRENE Onderzoeksprogramma*, Utrecht: Universiteit Utrecht.

Welenschappelijke Raad voor het Regeringsbeleid (WRR) (1992), *Milieubeleid: Strategie, Instrumenten en Handhaafbeleid*, The Hague: Sdu Uitgeverij (SDU).

4. Demand-side management (DSM)

Craig Mickle

INTRODUCTION

In a report published by the Office of Electricity Regulation (OFFER) in the UK, demand-side measures are defined as 'measures taken by an electricity supplier or other party (apart from the electricity consumer) to reduce a consumer's demand for electricity through improvements in the efficiency with which electricity is used'.[1] Demand-side measures should not be confused with energy conservation measures. The former differ from the latter in that economic cost-effectiveness tests are applied, and in that some demand-side measures may result in higher rather than lower energy consumption.[2] In this report we refer to these activities (from the provision of information, at one extreme, to direct utility – or third party – investment in improving their customers' energy efficiency, at the other), together with the process of determining which measures may be cost-effective, as demand-side management (DSM).

In order to shed light on the costs and benefits of DSM we need to identify exactly what we are talking about: the costs and benefits of DSM as a policy instrument; and/or the cost and benefits of particular DSM programmes. The first aspect of DSM relates to the *policies* used by government agencies to promote these practices by utilities (for example, whether by integrated resource planning (IRP) or by other techniques). Such regulatory policies are necessary to create a level playing field between the demand- and supply-side option, and may also be necessary to provide guidance to utility DSM. The second relates to the *practices* used by utilities in undertaking DSM.

This chapter deals with each of these areas in turn. First, it briefly describes the costs and benefits that may result from introducing changes in utility regulatory practices to allow DSM to compete effectively with the supply-side option, and steps that are being taken by European Union member states in this direction. Second, it looks at the costs and benefits of actual DSM programmes. In particular it analyses recent efforts in the EU in relation to domestic lighting programmes. The overall objective is to produce 'real' evidence of the costs and benefits of using DSM.

THE COSTS AND BENEFITS OF DSM AS A POLICY INSTRUMENT

The most important point to recognize about using DSM as a policy instrument is that in its purest form it is not simply a means of ensuring that energy efficiency schemes are undertaken. This is a mistaken 'conclusion' often drawn by both environmentalists (typically in favour of its adoption) and by utilities (often hostile to its introduction). The objective is not necessarily to ensure that utilities invest in improving their consumers' energy efficiency, but rather to ensure that it is an option that is considered. This has typically been interpreted as providing regulatory conditions under which the demand- and supply-side can be compared on a level playing field. In particular, this has meant removing the disincentives utilities have traditionally faced (primarily due to the way in which their revenue-earning capacity is regulated) and considering DSM as an alternative to increased supply.

There is considerable divergence in how far this process of removing disincentives has been taken, and how it has been done in North America. This is partly because agreement on how far it is necessary to go to create a level playing field is by no means universal. The main source of disagreement is over whether all consumers should pay for an energy efficiency programme, which in the short-term at least benefits the few. Some economists object to such an approach on the basis that, in their view, it involves 'cross-subsidization'. Others counter with the view that the situation is directly comparable with investments in supply. In general, however, many North American regulators have sought to ensure that within the definition of cost-effectiveness considered appropriate (often rejecting the former 'no-losers' argument), all DSM is pursued.

Introducing DSM as a policy instrument may impose various costs on society. These include the costs associated with changing price and other regulations where they discriminate against DSM, and the costs that DSM may involve in terms of uncertainty and regulatory risk. In the former case, to the extent that they can be separated from the regulatory costs associated with 'normal' change, these costs are likely to be small, one off and reflect technological development, new thinking and changing societal pressures.[3] In the latter case, introducing DSM may involve an increase in regulatory oversight which could in turn increase the return investors require. In the USA, for example, the integrated resource planning (IRP) framework tends to involve a significant degree of regulatory oversight. While it is by no means clear that the promotion of DSM requires that style of approach, some additional regulatory oversight is likely to be necessary for monitoring and evaluation. The extent of the increase in the regulatory burden will depend on what tests are applied in relation to cost-effectiveness and the extent to which the removal of disincentives and/or regulation is used to see this potential exploited.

In both cases the cost imposed needs to be weighed against the cost imposed by a system which may provide artificial incentives to the promotion of supply (or the benefit which will accrue when these are removed). Attempting to quantify these costs and benefits is extremely problematic and not possible in the context of this study. In California between 1990 and 1993, by the Public Utility Commission's (PUC) own reckoning, investor-owned utilities' energy efficiency programmes yielded their customers 'an estimated $1.9 billion (ECU1.57 billion) in lifecycle net resource benefits' after accounting for rebate and administrative expenses and all other utility and participant costs.[4,5] The California PUC is, however, debating wholesale changes to utility regulation along the lines of the UK model which, if implemented, would dramatically alter the utilities' incentives in relation to DSM.

Beyond efforts in North America there is very little experience which would provide a reliable indication of the 'real' costs of DSM as a policy instrument. To some extent, however, it could be expected that the costs of introducing DSM as a policy instrument would manifest themselves in the overheads incurred by a utility in complying with regulations and/or taking up the business opportunities offered in the new environment. Thus, they would be included when the cost-effectiveness of any DSM is considered.

The North American Approach

Much of the impetus for promoting DSM in North America has come through the adoption of IRP. IRP is a set of regulatory policies designed to ensure that energy utilities plan for and develop energy resources which are in the best economic interests of society. It is based on three fundamental principles:

- utilities should periodically conduct comprehensive assessments of *all* resource options available to meet customers' needs;
- satisfying customers' demand for electricity services through the promotion of efficient end-use devices is an alternative to electricity production; and
- the total costs and benefits of all resource options should be considered in order to determine the combination of resources that is in the best interests of all parties concerned: the utility, its consumers and society in general.

The specific IRP policies used in the USA vary considerably between different states. However, these policies all have the same general objectives, and there are certain critical elements used to achieve those objectives. In general, there are six such critical elements to IRP policies, described below.

These elements overlap in many ways, but are presented separately in order to clarify the most important aspects of IRP policies:

1. *Regulatory implementation of IRP*   IRP policies require the existence of a regulatory agency that has the authority and the mandate to establish and enforce IRP principles.
2. *Integrated resource plans*   The integrated resource plans are used to focus the debate on specific utility planning issues. The plans provide information to regulators regarding the utility's resource decisions; they allow for the regulators to provide feedback to the utility regarding those decisions; and they allow for the regulators to ensure that the utility's planning decisions are indeed in the best interests of the utility, its customers and society in general.
3. *Comparison of demand-side and supply-side resources*   IRP practices allow utilities to quantify the various cost and price impacts of DSM, in order to place them in perspective and to strike a balance between reducing overall costs and increasing electricity prices.
4. *Opening the electricity market to all suppliers of energy resources*   IRP also includes practices for purchasing power from independent (that is, non-utility) developers. Such practices allow utilities to take advantage of more diverse and possibly less expensive resources available from the electricity market, including customer generation, co-generation and renewable resources.
5. *Financial incentives for DSM*   Under traditional regulatory conditions, DSM is not always in a utility's best financial interest. Reduced electricity demand can lower a utility's revenues and profits. IRP addresses this problem by modifying regulatory conditions so that utilities can profit from successful DSM programmes. This allows utilities to adopt DSM resources as valid alternatives to supply-side resources and to incorporate them into their overall business strategies.
6. *Accounting for environmental externalities*   Some IRP policies promote a broad perspective which accounts for impacts on society as well as on utility customers. Environmental impacts are considered within this broader perspective via the use of externality adders when resource options are evaluated.

The European Approach

Whereas in North America the driving force behind the promotion of DSM was the realisation, in the wake of cost overruns on nuclear power stations in the 1970s, that reducing energy consumption may be a cheaper option, the impetus behind European interest in DSM has been primarily environmental.

The sort of detailed regulatory oversight and the legalistic nature of the regulatory system used in North America is alien to most European governments and cultures. In most member states governments have always been more heavily involved in utility planning, but in a more consensual framework (often through ownership of the utilities themselves – which is gradually changing). In some cases, governments have sought to play a more important role in promoting energy efficiency, particularly in northern Europe. Policies to encourage utilities to consider DSM are, however, evolving along a number of broad lines:

- levies are being used to raise the finance to fund DSM programme costs, without detailed reviews of, or modifications to, electricity tariffs (for example, in Denmark, Germany and the Netherlands);
- utility targets on emissions of greenhouse gases are being set. This effectively takes commitments on CO_2 as a new system constraint (similar to the Large Plant Combustion Directive or generation site approval), and allows utilities to achieve their existing goals within this framework. In what could be called 'environmental integrated resource planning', options for reducing CO_2 are ranked by their ability to meet an environmental target at the lowest cost (for example, in the Netherlands). This differs from conventional IRP where resources are ranked by their ability to provide electric capacity or energy at the lowest cost;
- changes are being made in the way revenues are earned in order to remove the disincentives faced by utilities in considering DSM. This basically includes measures that seek to 'decouple' utility profits from sales, thereby allowing the utility to pursue the options that are most cost-effective. The United Kingdom is one member state which is relying largely on this approach by altering price controls to remove any artificial incentives suppliers may have to favour increased supply.[6]

It should be noted that although the results from approaches may be the same (avoiding CO_2 emissions as cheaply as possible may result in cost-effective reductions in energy use), this may not always be the case. While the third approach mentioned above has perhaps most in common with DSM as it has developed in North America, all indirectly are attempting to deal with the key factor inhibiting the adoption of DSM, namely, financial disincentives.

The United Kingdom
In the United Kingdom the regulators of the electricity and gas industries have taken the first steps to ensure that the type of regulation used does not create inherent disincentives to the promotion of energy efficiency. This process has been aided by the restructuring that has occurred in these industries, and the

greater transparency in costs and prices this has allowed. As a result the UK is perhaps the member state that has done most in attempting to address the key underlying reasons why utility promotion of energy efficiency is inhibited.

This process has gone furthest in the electricity industry. It has occurred as the price controls which regulate the way the utilities earn revenue have been reviewed in their normal course. The regulator has considered the implications for energy efficiency when undertaking these reviews. All the key price controls in the electricity industry have been reviewed over the last three years.

Separate price controls distinguish between the regional electricity company (REC) supply business (potentially a competitive market) and distribution business (a monopoly market). The supply business involves the purchase of electricity for resale to end users. The supply price control covers the costs associated with the supply of electricity: primarily electricity purchase costs, but also costs associated with meter reading and billing.

The distribution business involves operating and maintaining the RECs' major asset: the distribution network. In order to recover the costs of undertaking these activities and to earn a return on the assets employed, the RECs charge customers (that is, those who use the network, regardless of who supplies them) fees for the use of the network. The distribution price control regulates these fees. The transmission price control operates on a similar basis and regulates the prices that can be charged for use of the high-voltage transmission network.

Under distribution price control, distribution revenue is collected on each unit of electricity sold, and is based on the average costs of operating the network. Distribution revenues increase, therefore, in direct proportion to sales.[7] The implicit assumption of this approach is that distribution *costs* increase in direct proportion to sales.

The regulator of the electricity industry has identified a significant proportion of costs which do not vary with the number of units sold, and has sought to introduce price controls to reflect this:

- In transmission he concluded that: 'The present control relates the maximum allowed revenue to a particular measure of the National Grid Company (NGC) activity (the number of units transmitted). However, within the period of the price control, NGC's costs are largely independent of this measure of activity, and over the longer term NGC's costs are driven as much or more by other factors' (OFFER, 1992, p. iii);
- in the supply business the Director General concluded that: 'Although some costs may be proportional to the number of kilowatt hours sold, a greater proportion is related to the number of customers. The proposed control assumes that about 25% of costs are kilowatt hour-related and about 75% customer-related' (OFFER, 1993b). Together with the fixed term,

the unit-related term in the new supply price control is about one-fifth of its previous level;

* in distribution he concluded that: 'On the evidence available to me it does not seem that distribution costs can be said to move entirely with units sold. At the same time, I am conscious of the importance of retaining a general incentive for companies to seek out and meet the needs of their customers. To balance these considerations, I propose to halve from 100% to 50% the weight of units in the revenue driver of the price control, and to relate the remaining 50% to customer numbers' (OFFER, 1994b, pp. 33–4). This would imply that the costs that do vary with the number of units sold are significantly less than 50 per cent.

The idea is that with cost-reflective price controls and competition in supply the disincentives to energy efficiency will be removed. While it is by no means clear that the regulator's decision in relation to the distribution price control removes all the artificial incentive to the promotion of increased supply as opposed to reduced demand, it is certainly a step in the right direction. Because customers in the under 100 kW market remain in the franchise market and are not yet able to choose their supplier, the regulator has included an allowance of £100 million over four years (approximately £1 per customer per year) to be spent on improving the efficiency with which electricity is used. He has also introduced standards of performance to ensure that this money is spent cost-effectively (although it is not clear why these would be necessary if the disincentives to energy efficiency had been fully removed, as is claimed).

The Energy Saving Trust (EST) is an organization created by the government and owned by it and the gas and electricity industries. It has been given the job by government of achieving 25 per cent of the UK's overall CO_2 reduction target and was to finance this by a levy on domestic consumers' gas and electricity bills (similar to the Dutch approach). Both regulators have stated their unwillingness to raise the funds necessary (the EST suggests that in order to meet its target it would need to be spending roughly £400 million per annum in the latter years of the century), which they say should be raised through general fiscal policy.

On the basis of the above it is not possible to form a conclusion regarding the 'real' costs and benefits of DSM as a policy instrument. This will depend very much on the approach adopted; given the lack of experience in these matters, it may be some time before the costs and benefits become fully apparent. The differences between the approaches adopted suggest that there may be significant variation in their costs and that political involvement will inevitably interfere with the solutions. A solution based more on dealing with the inherent disincentives generated by typical types of utility regulation would, however, appear to offer a relatively low-cost way to proceed. The basic lesson is then perhaps that creating a level playing field need not be expensive, although in practice it may well be.

THE COSTS AND BENEFITS OF DSM PROGRAMMES

There are a number of costs and benefits associated with actual DSM programmes, which will vary in size and scope depending on the nature of the DSM programme undertaken (that is, whether it involves information only, subsidy and so on). It should be pointed out, however, that just how cost-effective DSM programmes are in North America (where most of the relevant experience is to date) is an area of some controversy and continuing debate (see Joskow, 1994; Lovins, 1994). This is partly because of disagreements about which costs and benefits should be included, and partly due to the problems associated with evaluation of DSM.

In general, DSM costs include the utility's investments necessary to purchase, market, deliver and install energy efficiency measures. The benefits include the electricity generation, transmission and distribution costs that are avoided by the DSM programme. These costs and benefits can accrue to different parties (that is, the customer, a utility/producer, society); be 'real' (in the cash flow sense) or implied (for example, time, hassle); and vary in the extent to which they can be quantified (such as, equipment cost or environmental benefits).

It must be said that many of the less direct costs and benefits are difficult to measure because they are hard to observe and vary widely across consumers. As such, they are best discussed in relation to particular programmes, as is done below. This section merely serves to outline briefly their nature and scope.

DSM programmes are considered 'cost-effective' as long as they cost less than the electricity that they displace.[8] The net result of implementing cost-effective DSM programmes is to reduce the total costs of meeting customers' demand for energy services. In practice, to look at the costs and benefits of DSM programmes is, when society's viewpoint is considered, no different from assessing the cost-effectiveness of any schemes to promote energy efficiency. In the case of DSM, however, it is typically a utility rather than a government agency which is responsible for implementation. Those analysed in this report involve, to varying degrees, utilities and government agencies.

The Costs of DSM Programmes

The *direct* costs of specific conservation measures include the cost of the equipment and its installation, regardless of how those costs are shared between the utility and the participating customer. They should also include any maintenance and operating costs incurred by the participating customer. Taxes are excluded on both energy and equipment as these are transfer payments.

The *indirect* costs of the programme include the administrative costs of operating the programme (that is, the costs of auditing, advertising, marketing, other promotional expenses, and monitoring and evaluation). In addition, it may also be appropriate to include a share of the utilities' general overheads to DSM programmes (such as the costs of general information programmes, office space and administrative support, planning, executive time, legal and regulatory costs) (see Joskow, 1994).[9]

There are also a number of other costs which, although often difficult to quantify because they are implied rather than real, should not be completely ignored. This includes the customer's transaction costs (that is, any time spent shopping, filling out energy surveys, dealing with plumbers, carpenters, electricians and contractors). It also includes the value of any lost business and the cost of any inconvenience incurred while the measures are being installed.

There is also a cost involved where those who would have purchased the efficient technology in any case have received an unnecessary subsidy (for example, so-called free-riders). As this is already reflected in the real cost that has been incurred in operating the programme (which would otherwise have to be artificially lowered), it is accounted for in the analysis in this report by making a corresponding reduction in the programme benefits (such as net energy savings). These can be significant.

Other costs may include any secondary impact on energy consumption as a result of interactions between energy consumption in different end uses (for example, the effect more efficient lighting may have on heat and/or air conditioning consumption). There may also be some 'snapback': the tendency of the consumer to demand more energy service from more efficient appliances (or to use them 'improperly'), which again is handled as a reduction in the net benefits.[10] Finally, any cost associated with bringing forward the disposal of the existing appliance should also be included.

The Benefits of DSM Programmes

The *direct* benefits of specific conservation measures include the avoided cost of the displaced generation, regardless of how those benefits are shared between the participating customer, the utility, non-participating customers and society at large. An assessment of the avoidable costs of UK electricity is presented in the appendix. The most obvious of these are the avoided costs of electricity supply both in energy terms (kWh) and in terms of avoided capacity costs (kW – in generation, transmission or distribution). These benefits may vary depending upon the time frame considered, particularly in relation to capacity savings. It should be noted that, due to the way they are typically charged for electricity consumption, the avoided cost for the participating customer is likely to be greater than the avoided cost from society's or the industry's perspective (in fact, creating a perverse incentive to energy efficiency which is accounted for when taking society's perspective).[11] The direct benefits should also include any costs the participating customer can avoid in relation to capital, maintenance and operating costs.

The *external* benefits of the programme are those that accrue to society. Some of these can be quantified directly (they should be similar to the utility's avoided costs, and include avoided transmission and distribution losses), while others (mainly environmental benefits, but also employment and health) require some willingness to pay or other pricing mechanism in order to be quantified because they are not currently monetized. Both of these rely crucially on the assessment of avoided kWh and kW mentioned above, an area where evaluation is critical.

To establish the avoided kWh of a DSM programme requires two stages. First, as was mentioned above, it must be established how many consumers were actually stimulated to act because of the programme. Therefore it is appropriate to net out any free-riders and 'free-drivers' (see below). Second, to establish the average usage patterns of the more efficient appliances installed as a result of the programme, snapback and any other losses (for example, from transmission and distribution) need to be accounted for.

There may also be a number of other (real) benefits of DSM programmes. Manufacturers will often offer the products at a cheaper price if higher volumes are guaranteed (whilst they save on distribution and promotion costs) as a result of a programme. As this is a real saving in the cost of the programme it is accounted for amongst the costs in the analysis in this report. In addition, if the programme leads to permanently higher volumes, then price reductions may hold after the subsidy period has finished, promoting further sales. Alternately, some consumers may be stimulated to purchase the appliance as a result of the campaign but not receive the subsidy, particularly where rebates are involved (so-called free-drivers). Furthermore, once the more efficient product has been used, there is a higher probability of replacement purchase. These are not uncommon phenomena.

The customer may also be able to avoid some (implied) transaction costs as a result of the programme; indeed, overcoming consumers' apparently high transaction costs is the key to the cost-effectiveness of many programmes. The savings in transaction costs are the reductions in time and hassle related to help with installation, reduction in repeat purchases, and/or saving in maintenance and disposal costs (with certain technologies these could represent additional costs). These other benefits, although more uncertain and difficult to quantify, can be of considerable importance (Lovins, 1994).

THE COSTS AND BENEFITS OF DOMESTIC LIGHTING PROGRAMMES

Lighting Use and Electricity Demand

Lighting is a significant end-use of electricity. Demand for lighting accounts for some 9–18 per cent of all electricity demand in IEA countries (IEA, 1989). In the EU, lighting accounts for (very) roughly 8 per cent of total electricity consumption, which breaks down into 7 per cent of domestic electricity sales; 6 per cent of industrial electricity sales; and about 15 per cent of tertiary sector electricity consumption.[12] In the USA, by contrast, lighting accounts for some 17 per cent of total electricity demand and in the UK for roughly 15 per cent of total electricity consumption (see EPRI, 1993; ACE, 1993). The variation in the UK and EU estimates is difficult to account for and probably says more about the state of knowledge of electricity end-use in Europe than about actual consumption.

Lighting is a popular option for DSM programmes. In the USA, for example, it is predicted that by 2000 the cumulative impact of lighting programmes will be avoided electricity consumption of some 40 TWh (terawatt hours) (see Table 4.1). Indeed, some 29 per cent of all US DSM programmes (by anticipated savings) are directed towards the end use of lighting, much higher than its proportional contribution to total electricity sales. Commercial lighting programmes are the single most important area of DSM in the USA.

Table 4.1   DSM impacts by end-use market in the USA

Programme type	Cumulative DSM impacts by 2000		Summer peak		Winter peak	
	TWh	%	GW	%	GW	%
Commercial lighting	33.37	24	7.34	14	5.01	12
Domestic lighting .	6.92	5	0.53	1	1.22	3
Total lighting	40.29	29	7.87	15	6.23	15
Total all DSM	140.68		51.59		41.24	

Source: EPRI (1993).

Lighting is a popular end-use for DSM programmes for several reasons. First, and most important, is the fact that despite more energy-efficient technologies having been commercially available for over a decade and their seemingly attractive economics (see below), the market penetration of compact fluorescent lamps (CFL) is low.

The technical and *prima facie* economic potential of more efficient lighting is considerable. CFL typically require 80 per cent less electricity per unit of light output. The higher first cost of CFL is typically paid back in energy savings in a time period of roughly two years. The IEA identifies an overall 'commercially feasible' savings opportunity to reduce the electricity used by lighting by more than 50 per cent on a national scale (IEA, 1989, p. 70; as reported in Mills, 1996). In addition to the energy savings, lighting programmes can offer significant capacity savings. In short, the benefits of improved lighting (in terms of avoided costs) tend to be large in relation to other energy-efficiency options.

Lighting programmes are also popular because of the stand-alone nature of the end-use, which ensures that lighting programmes tend to be relatively simple to design and implement and inexpensive to run (Oak Ridge National Laboratory, 1989). In short, the costs also tend to be modest relative to other DSM programmes.

Experience with EU Lighting Programmes

Efforts to improve the take-up of more efficient lighting have been at the forefront of European utilities' first DSM programmes. Work has been undertaken by Mills (1991a) to assess the first of these efforts. His conclusions are summarized over in Box 4.1.

The cost-effectiveness of the lighting programmes was computed in terms of the cost of conserved energy (CCE) to all parties, that is, the direct costs per unit of energy saved plus indirect costs such as those for administration, marketing and evaluation/surveys, annualized using a 6 per cent real discount rate and no taxes. Based on consumer surveys, average lamp operation time is assumed to be four hours a day.

Mills notes that non-participants sometimes benefited because increases in lamp sales due to the programmes encouraged manufacturers to lower normal retail prices:

> In Denmark, for example, prices fell from 300 Dkr (ECU40) in 1987 to 125 Dkr (ECU17) in 1991, excluding the effects of inflation. Importantly, despite the cost of marketing CFLs under the programmes, the programmes achieved substantially *lower* overall societal costs of conserved energy than would have been the case if consumers had bought the lamps on their own. This is due to the low prices that utilities obtained when co-operating with lighting vendors or when buying lamps in large quantities. Utilities obtained prices that were about one-third to one-quarter of the prevailing market prices. (Mills, 1991a, p. 129)[13]

The cost-effectiveness of some programmes was boosted by an increase in the sales of CFL to non-participants. For example: 'According to Dutch utilities the GEB programme resulted in 25 000 direct sales versus 50 000 indirect sales.

Box 4.1
Evaluation of compact fluorescent light (CFL) promotion campaigns in Europe

'Between late-1987 and mid-1991, many electric utilities in Europe offered financial incentives to promote the use of CFLs. At least 51 programmes have taken place in 10 countries: Austria, Denmark, Finland, Germany, Ireland, Italy, the Netherlands, Sweden, Switzerland, and the United Kingdom. About 7.2 million households have been eligible for the programmes, acquiring about 2.2 million CFLs. For the seven countries (39 programmes) where data were available, the average societal cost of the energy saved in the programmes was 2.1 cents/kWh (22 mECU/kWh),[a] including 0.3 cents/kWh for programme administration and marketing. This is very cost-effective from the societal perspective, i.e. approximately one-third the cost of building and operating new electric power plants. Some of the programmes have been available to non-residential customers.

'Post-programme surveys contain a significant amount of useful information on programme impacts, customer response, and broader market response. Key findings include:

- the most societally cost-effective programmes resulted when utilities paid a high proportion (or all) of the cost of the efficient lamps,
- consumer penetration correlates very weakly with the level of incentives,
- information-only programmes achieved the lowest penetration rates,
- the form of the incentive is an important determinant of participation,
- non-economic factors are at least as important as economic factors in determining participation,
- women and men respond differently to lighting programmes,
- pensioners and occupants of single-family homes are over-represented as programme participants in relation to their representation in the total eligible populations,
- consumer self-reported interest in buying CFLs is highly sensitive to lamp prices, with a strong increase in interest at a price of about $10 to $15 (7 to 10 ECU/lamp), and
- the use of CFLs is highly coincident with periods of peak utility demand.'

Note: [a] In this report, mECU refers to ECU divided by 1000. The conversion relates to the exchange rate at the time the report was written (1991). All figures taken from research by Mills have used the exchange rate from that report. As regards the rest of this report, exchange rates for mid-December 1994 have been used.

Source: Mills (1991a).

The corresponding numbers for the first Dutch Friesland utility programme were 60 000 and 40 000 CFLs. In Switzerland, 7000 CFLs were sold because of the programme and 'normal' sales increased by 70 000' (ibid., p. 132).

Programme evaluations also show a modest degree of incorrect or inefficient use of CFL and increased use in some programmes (reducing savings by about 5 per cent), all of which tend to reduce programme cost-effectiveness (ibid., p. 133). Mills also notes that in comparison to US programmes, European programmes typically have had more direct and active manufacturer involvement, higher consumer participation rates and lower costs of conserved energy. Government involvement has also been greater. On the other hand, marketing tends to be more naive in Europe.

These evaluations highlight the importance of the form of incentive, as opposed to its size, for example, merely enabling consumers to pay their bills often results in higher participation rates. Further work by Wilms (of Philips Lighting) and Mills has analysed the price and non-price factors influencing the adoption of CFL in light of 'the nearly complete lack of correlation between CFL price and consumer response rates for a number of programmes' (Wilms and Mills, 1993). They conclude that programme design must be sensitive to non-price factors to maximize cost-effectiveness, and emphasize the importance of proper market analysis and segmentation.

COST/BENEFIT ANALYSIS OF RECENT EU DOMESTIC LIGHTING PROGRAMMES

In this section we analyse a number of programmes which have operated in various member states in an attempt to quantify their costs and benefits.

Austria

The only domestic lighting programme operated in Austria to date (as far as it has been possible to ascertain) was a three-month initiative run by KELAG, a generation and distribution company, in the Province of Carinthia (see Mills, 1993). This was a partially manufacturer-funded rebate programme which encouraged consumers to purchase up to two CFL. Of the 116 000 eligible households, 14 274 (12 per cent) participated. According to Mills, the costs of conserved energy (CCE) of the programme was some 32 mECU/kWh saved, which is 45 per cent higher than the average cost of the programmes surveyed.

France

It appears that there have been a few domestic lighting programmes in France. Efforts to curb electricity demand on the French islands to delay/avoid investment on the supply side have involved lighting programmes. Some pilot projects have also been operated on the mainland. Most of these programmes have been undertaken only recently and, as a result, little information is as yet available regarding cost-effectiveness.

Germany

There have been a number of domestic lighting programmes in Germany. Mills (1993) describes a three-month programme operated by Energie-Versorgungsunternehmen Schwaben, a generation and distribution utility. A rebate scheme was used to encourage householders to purchase one CFL. Of the 800 000 eligible households, some 61 000 (8 per cent) participated. According to Mills, the CCE of the programme was some 19 mECU/kWh saved, slightly lower than the average cost of the programmes in the survey.

According to Vereinigung Deutscher Elektrizitätswerke (VDEW – the Association of German Utilities), a number of utilities are embarking on lighting programmes. Typically these are run by regional or local utilities, making data collection difficult in the context of this study (sketchy details on a couple of these programmes are outlined below). The VDEW concludes that: 'DSM projects in Germany are primarily pilot projects of which concrete results of evaluation are not yet available.'[14]

The Government of Schleswig Holstein operated a lighting programme for public buildings, financed by the utility VEBA. It resulted in a 'poor' cost-benefit ratio as a result of inadequate and poorly targeted marketing, lack of direct utility involvement, high administrative costs and a lack of planning (see Morovic, 1993). The author notes that many of these obstacles could have been overcome with better planning and organization. It is also concluded that, given all the problems, the programme yielded far better results than might have been expected (that is, a relatively high penetration rate with what appeared to be significant additional market stimulus).

Stadtwerke Saarbrücken recently ran a CFL free give away/direct installation programme. The campaign had expected a penetration rate of 25–30 per cent. In all, 20 000 CFL will be distributed, saving some 8 million kWh over the next eight years, at an expected cost of 0.06–0.08 DM/kWh (0.032–0.042 ECU/kWh).[15] The City of Langenhagen in 1992 carried out a CFL programme, with a cost of 0.063 DM/kWh (0.033 ECU/kWh) saved.[16]

Ireland

A pilot scheme was conducted in 1990 by the Electricity Supply Board (see Mills, 1993). It offered householders up to four CFL with a discount and pay-on-your-bill offers and was part-sponsored by manufacturers. Of the 25 000 eligible households, some 5000 (20 per cent) participated in the programme. According to Mills (ibid.), the CCE of the programme was some 46.5 mECU/kWh saved, which is double the average cost of the programmes in the survey.

The Netherlands

Of the countries examined in this study, the Netherlands has undertaken the largest and most widespread efforts to improve the efficiency of lighting. Mills (1993) summarizes the results of a number of programmes operated by utilities in 1988–9. These involved a variety of rebate programmes with the support of manufacturers, retailers and government. Of the 3 150 000 eligible households, some 1 173 375 (37 per cent) chose to participate, purchasing on average 2.5 CFL per household. According to Mills, the average CCE of these programmes was some 19.3 mECU/kWh saved, which is below the average cost of the programmes in the survey.

The role for the promotion of energy efficiency has expanded since the publication in 1990 of the Dutch government's plans in relation to reducing greenhouse gases (Ministry of Economic Affairs, 1990).[17] The Dutch approach to improving the efficiency of energy use is embodied in its National Environmental Energy Plan Plus (NEEP+) and *Energy Conservation Memorandum*.

The National Energy-Economy Lamp Campaign has set a target of an average of 3.5 energy-efficient lamps per household by 1995; its objective is to reduce electricity consumption by 25 per cent from this effort. The distribution utilities, which have a key role in the government's plans, believe that before the year 2000 they can encourage the replacement of 15 million light bulbs with the same number of energy-efficient lamps.[18] It should be noted that the main driver behind these schemes is the commitment to reduce greenhouse gas emissions, as opposed to cost-effectiveness (see above, pp. 74–5).[19]

As a result of this plan many of the 30 or so Dutch regional distribution utilities are at various stages of implementing lighting programmes. Unfortunately, this makes tracking their costs and benefits a time-consuming exercise.

A summary of the Nationale Spaarlampenactie 1993–4 (national CFL campaign) has been put together by EnergieNed (the association of energy distribution companies). This covers activity in this area between 15 September 1993 and 2 March 1994. During this period, sales of CFL were 3 000 000, of which roughly 2 000 000 were not replacements. The total penetration of CFL has reached 14 000 000, which is 2.22 per household (up from 1.76 in 1993). Some 55.7 per cent of households now have one or more CFL. This is up from 40 per cent in October 1991, when the number per household was 1.1 (EnergieNed, 1994).

Until recently, subsidies in addition to bill-paying mechanisms have been used more widely. In this recent campaign, however, advertising and promotion have been the main tools; very few distribution companies have been willing to offer subsidies. There are a number of reasons for this: while subsidies played an important role in increasing market penetration and reducing CFL prices (in the early phase of the campaign), more recently they have not produced the further reductions in prices the distribution companies thought feasible. Subsidies have thus come to be seen as primarily for the producer, as opposed to the customer. The distribution companies also believe they have captured most of the consumers who are likely to be attracted to CFL by the subsidy. They are now attempting to attract those who will purchase for other reasons. The marketing campaign is therefore being directed towards promoting these benefits, including such things as sales promotion, for example, through competitions.

Because of these factors (the overlap in different energy efficiency campaigns, the diversity of methods used, and the length of its operation), a true analysis of cost-effectiveness would need to look at the cost and benefits of the campaign as a whole. This is beyond the scope of this chapter.

The national cost of the 1993–4 programme – primarily for publicity – was Fl5.35 million (ECU2.5 million) of which the national government paid Fl1million (ECU0.47 million), the participating producers Fl1.5 million (ECU0.7 million), and EnergieNed the rest.[20] The cost of the regional activities is difficult to estimate because of their number, the discrepancy in the approaches used, and the difficulty in separating out what costs should be allocated to lighting programmes as opposed to some of their other energy-saving initiatives. As a guesstimate EnergieNed suggests that the total expenditure on the programme attributable to the non-replacement sales (including that of the distribution companies) was Fl4.7 million (ECU2.2 million).[21] With estimated annual savings of 35 kWh/annum (for 600 hours use per annum) or 467 kWh over the product's lifetime, the total savings will be 934 GWh. The cost per kWh saved is some Fl0.005 /kWh (ECU0.0023 /kWh). If customer costs are assumed to be of the order of those of the Amsterdam lighting programmes (see below), then the average cost of the whole programme CCE would be ECU0.024 /kWh.

The withdrawal of subsidies has not seen a reduction in CFL sales; indeed, according to EnergieNed, sales have increased slightly on their previous trend rate with the new approach. As a result, they are satisfied with the result, although it may indicate the existence of some free-riders when subsidies were being offered.

Energiebedrijf Amsterdam (EBA) currently operates domestic and service sector lighting programmes. In its 1993 domestic programme some 20 000 CFL were sold, leading to an estimated 47 kWh/annum reduction in electricity demand per lamp, or 7 520 000 kWh over their life. With total programme costs of some Fl547 361 (ECU256 616), the savings cost some Fl0.0728/kWh (ECU0.034/kWh) saved.[22] This is much higher than the cost of the Mills programme, but still lower than avoided costs.

The United Kingdom

Manweb's Holyhead Power Save scheme

Manweb plc is a regional electricity company (owner of the distribution network and a supplier) serving Merseyside and North Wales. In December 1992 it launched 'Power Save', a project designed to assess the impact on electricity consumption of a large-scale energy-efficiency initiative. The site chosen was the town of Holyhead, a remote town on Holy Island adjacent to the island of Anglesey off the north-west coast of Wales. Holyhead was chosen because of its size and the ease with which its power consumption could be monitored on the network (demand is monitored every half-hour), and also because of the opportunity it provided for delaying investment in the distribution grid supplying the town (Manweb, 1993b).

Currently Holyhead is served by two 33 000-volt transformers which are in danger of becoming overloaded. Under the business-as-usual scenario, electricity demand from Holyhead is set to rise by 2 per cent per annum, which would require a £750 000 (ECU966 744) investment in the distribution network (within two years) to uprate its link to Anglesey.[23]

The objective is to reduce Holyhead's peak electricity demand of around 9 MW to 8 MW within six months (or by 11 per cent: enough to supply 1000 homes) on a sustainable basis, making this one of the largest projects of its type undertaken in Europe (Manweb, 1993a). All energy users in Holyhead are being targeted. This includes 3500 homes, 623 commercial customers and 37 industrial energy users. The scheme has put into place an extensive programme of information on saving electricity and special offers on energy-saving measures and appliances.

Domestic consumers have been given special attention because they account for 51 per cent of consumption in the area. Lighting is a major initiative in this sector (see below). Other initiatives include free lagging on hot water cylinders for those who use immersion heaters as their main source of water heating, and discounted (£16 or ECU20.6) loft insulation and light-proofing. As many domestic appliances were found to be over 15 years old, householders were encouraged to replace them with the offer of substantial refunds (for example, fridges, washing machines, dish washers).[24]

These campaigns have been supported by an extensive marketing effort which involved leaflets, advertising and surveys. Manweb has also managed to enlist the help and support of a number of voluntary and government organizations including an £80 000 (ECU103 119) grant from the EU's SAVE programme. The total investment in the project is some £500 000 (ECU644 496).[25] Monitoring is to continue for at least two years, with particular emphasis on winter periods in order to achieve a meaningful comparison with existing records. RAF Valley, Anglesey's air base, continues to provide meteorological data so that figures can be weather-corrected for a true comparison.

The costs of the domestic lighting programme   Manweb pinpointed the hall and landing, lounge and kitchen as the three areas where lighting is most used. A number of special offers were made to help customers reduce consumption. Each home was offered two energy-saving light bulbs for the price of two ordinary light bulbs: £1.40 (ECU1.8). CFL were discounted from £11 (ECU14.2) each, their recommended retail price, to 70 pence (ECU0.9) each. The cost of the programme was reduced because of the £4.50 (ECU5.8) discount offered by Philips to the utility purchase. In other words, the utility paid the difference between the £6.50 (ECU8.38) cost of the CFL and the customer price of 70 pence.

The CFL which were offered last eight times as long and use only 20 per cent of the power of the conventional general lighting service (GLS) they replace and have a similar warm colour appearance (Manweb, 1993a). To ease the purchase process Manweb offered forms which could be filled in and would result in a visit from a Manweb representative to install the bulbs. Alternatively the free telephone service mentioned above was made available. As a result of these actions 78 per cent of households took up the offer.[26]

Despite these efforts to reduce the transaction costs associated with participation in the scheme, some of the consumer's time and attention was still required. These were presumably enough to dissuade some of those 22 per cent who did not participate. According to post-programme research conducted by the utility, one of the key reasons put forward by these customers was ignorance of the offer. The fact that there are transaction costs associated with these types of programme is illustrated by the fact that different customers responded differently to the free installation offer (60 per cent refused it). Intrusion into the home may well be a significant transaction cost. In contrast to what could be expected in relation to transaction costs (that is, that it would be harder to engage the participation of wealthier customers), the opposite was found to be the case in Holyhead. Wealthier customers, however, were more inclined than poorer customers to move CFL to areas that may not be used as frequently at peak periods, for example, bathrooms (see below). Typically it was wealthier households (relative to the average in Holyhead) who favoured the free installation offer. (It was speculated that this may be due to the higher likelihood of one member of the family being at home.)

As it is difficult to quantify these costs and benefits reliably (short of conducting time and motion studies), it is assumed, for the purpose of our cost-effectiveness analysis, that the transaction costs incurred as a result of participating are equal to those avoided as a result of participating. (The avoided capital costs of the CFL are included in the benefits discussed below.)[27]

This is a prudent and, in all likelihood, conservative assumption. It should be noted, however, that these costs and benefits, although difficult to quantify, are unlikely to be insignificant, as the illustration below shows.[28] Indeed, the absence of accounting for the customer's transaction cost in many US utilities' programme evaluations is one of the key criticisms of the cost-effectiveness estimates made by them and of the cost-effectiveness of the programmes themselves (Joskow, 1994).[29]

While the utility may have reduced the consumer's transaction costs by the actions that it has undertaken (see Box), in the process it has incurred some administrative and overhead costs – *indirect* programme costs – itself. These are estimated on the basis of discussions with Manweb and are illustrated in

---

Box 4.2

Transaction costs of participating in a demand-side management programme: illustration

It is assumed that to participate in the programme required 30 minutes of the participant's time. At the opportunity cost wage of roughly £18 000 per annum (or ECU23 202) this equates to roughly ECU13.8 per hour.[a] The transaction costs would have then been ECU6.9 per household, or ECU18 837 (some 12 per cent of total programme costs).

If it is also assumed that the repurchase, installation and disposal of the GLS takes ten minutes, then with seven replacements the total time taken would be 70 minutes. In nominal terms this would represent a transaction cost of some ECU16.1 per household, or ECU13.05 per household in present value terms. In total this would increase the benefits of the programme by ECU35 627.

The net effect therefore of these other costs as a result of the programme would be an increase of the net benefits by some ECU16 790. In the case of Holyhead, in a very depressed region of the UK, £18 000 is unlikely to be a realistic estimate of the annual average opportunity cost of a person's time. This will reduce both the (transaction) cost and the benefits of the programme. Manweb suggest a figure of £11 000 may be more appropriate for the region. This would reduce the net benefit to ECU10 000.

Note:[a]   ECU13.8 per hour @ 48 weeks and 35 hours per week. 'The Legal and General Insurance Company regularly estimates the replacement cost of a spouse as houshold manager, for insurance purposes. In 1993 the figure was £18,000, well above average earnings that year in Britain.' (Charles Handy, *The Empty Raincoat: Making Sense of the Future*, London: Hutchinson, 1994, p. 185).

Table 4.2.[30] For the domestic lighting aspect of the overall initiative, the overhead cost (including general overheads) was some £90 000 (ECU116 009).

This is indeed a high figure (being double the equipment cost). Manweb suggests, however, that this is the first time it had undertaken such an exercise and that it therefore had to do everything from scratch. In addition, it took the approach that this was a learning exercise and was therefore prepared to undertake considerable analysis to work out how well the programme was working (see below). This figure does not include any of the costs of the voluntary bodies that participated in the programme (and did a proportion of the administrative work) or any of the subsidy offered by the EU to help fund the programme.[31] Manweb is confident that if it were to undertake a similar initiative again these costs would be substantially reduced. In addition, it believes that the programme has been very good from a public relations perspective, as it has noticed a very positive shift in customer attitudes towards the company. All the aspects of programme costs are illustrated in Table 4.2.

The benefits of the domestic lighting programme   Establishing the benefits (that is, the costs avoided) of the programme requires a very close analysis of the precise effects it had. First, any outside influences on the number of participants must be netted out, subtracting any free-riders (those who were unnecessary recipients of the subsidy because they would have purchased the CFL in any case) and adding in any free-drivers (those who have been encouraged to purchase CFL as a result of the programme). In this example there is no evidence of a significant number of free-riders: sales of CFL before the programme were almost zero in Holyhead. There has been some free-driver effect, however. The only distributor on the island has seen a modest increase in CFL since the programme was undertaken. This has, however, been difficult to quantify and therefore it is assumed to be zero. The private benefits of the programme are the avoided electricity purchases made by the participants and the avoided replacement purchases of GLS.

A critical variable determining the effectiveness of the CFL in reducing electricity consumption is where they are installed. As a result, Manweb spent a considerable amount of effort to ensure that they were installed in areas where most electricity was used, particularly at peak periods. The evidence suggests that lower-income households were more prepared to leave them in the 'right' places than were higher-income households, some of whom preferred to use them in other applications (for example, porch lights). As Manweb's sole interest in the programme was how well it could reduce peak demand, this is where its post-programme evaluation efforts focused. These efforts suggest that about 50 per cent of bulbs have drifted from the peak demand lighting points in which Manweb was most interested. Manweb also suggests that the 20W CFL replaced on average a 70W bulb. It has been assumed for the purpose of this

Table 4.2 *Manweb DSM programme costs (ECU)*

Year	Penetration rate (%)	No. of CFL packs sold	Equipment cost			Total	Customer			Utility		Society Admin. costs	Total programme costs
			Customer	Utility	Plus producer discount		Transaction	Installing/ main.	Total customer costs	Admin./ customer overheads	Total utility cost		
0	78	2 730	4 927	40 820	31 671	77 417	0	0	4 927	116 010	156 830	0	161 757

Table 4.3 *Manweb DSM programme benefits (ECU)*

Year	No. of participants	Less free riders	Add free drivers	Net participants	Private benefits						Society			
					Annual electricity savings (MWh)	Avoided costs (mECU /kWh)	Electricity cost savings	Avoided repurchases	Avoided transaction cost	Avoided main./ disposal	Avoided cost (mECU /kWh)	Total avoided electricity costs	Other avoided costs	Total avoided costs
0	2 730	0	0	2 730	399	11.92	47 510	4 927	0	0	3.70	14 745	4 927	19 672
1					399	11.92	47 510	4 927			3.70	14 745	4 927	19 672
2					399	11.92	47 510	9 853			3.70	14 745	9 853	24 598
3					399	11.92	47 510	4 927			3.70	14 745	4 927	19 672
4					399	11.92	47 510	9 853			3.70	14 745	9 853	24 598
5					191	11.92	22 779	0			3.70	7 070	0	7 070
Total				2 184			260 326	34 486	0	0		80 796	34 486	115 281
Present value							229 157	30 285				71 122	30 285	101 406

Notes:

Units: mECU in this case are ECU divided by 100.

Private benefits: The avoided costs are the normal domestic rate per kWh of electricity supplied (7.87p/kWh); Electricity cost savings are the annual electricity savings multiplied by the avoided costs; Avoided re-purchases is the number of participants multiplied by the avoided cost of repurchase. This assumes that the CFL will last 8,000 hours (or 5.5 years with four hours use a day) as compared with 1,000 hours for the incandescent. It has been assumed that the existing light had a full life left, so only seven additional purchases are counted.

Society: The societal avoided cost is derived from Appendix One and is 0.037 ECU/kWh or 3.7 mECU/kWh.

analysis that the average daily use of the CFL was four hours. Manweb has suggested that in terms of kW reductions it has assumed that only those in the correct applications will be considered as 'sustained'. This is an assumption, but is partially supported by discussions it has had with the Electricity Supply Board (ESB) in Ireland, who undertook lighting load research.

The assumption about avoided replacement costs is that the CFL will last 8000 hours (or 5.5 years with four hours' use a day) as compared with 1000 hours for the incandescent bulbs. It has been assumed that the existing light had a full life left, so only seven additional purchases are counted.

For the purpose of the cost-benefit calculation it is assumed that the avoided cost of electricity generation is ECU3.7 per kWh (see the appendix for the derivation of this figure). On this basis, the benefits of the programme are equal to ECU101 406 in present value terms, as illustrated in Table 4.3.

There would also have been some other benefits to society in terms of the avoided/delayed cost of upgrading the network. Manweb's original estimate of the utility cost of upgrading the network was £750 000. Although the lighting programme proved to be an expensive method of reducing peak demand in relation to its other programmes, it clearly provided some benefits to society. However, because of the uncertainty associated with calculating these society benefits, they have been assumed to be zero.

Cost-effectiveness   Table 4.4 summarizes the result of the programme. It suggests that the domestic lighting programme itself was almost certainly not cost-effective from society's viewpoint. To provide further indications of its cost-effectiveness a number of figures which show the cost in kWh and kW terms of new combined cycle gas turbines (CCGT) which, in practice, represent the most likely generation alternative at the present time.

Table 4.4   Net present value of DSM programme

Total benefits	101 406
Total costs	161 577
Net present value	−60 350
Benefit: cost ratio	0.6
Energy savings (mECU/kWh)	
DSM costs	7.4
Net saving	−3.7
Cost-low	3.1
Cost-high	4.9
Capacity savings (ECU/kW)	
DSM costs	1 185
CCGT cost[a]	499

Note: [a]   CCGT = combined-cycle gas turbine.

It should be noted, however, that Manweb has concluded that the project as a whole has been a major success as a pilot project, achieving the targeted 10 per cent peak demand reduction (Manweb, 1994). The average cost per kilovolt ampere (kVA) saved was £291 overall (ECU375/kVA). This is significantly lower than the avoided cost of new CCGT.[32]

In the domestic sector, which accounted for 30 per cent of the savings, the cost was £512/kVA (ECU660). The industrial sector initiatives cost only £126 kVA (ECU162), and were responsible for 57 per cent of the savings.

Environmental Benefits   Table 4.5 shows schematically the environmental benefits of the programme. It assumes that coal is the marginal plant (as indeed it generally is in the UK at the moment), although this may change for certain periods of the year as more CCGT capacity comes on line. The values in ECU/g of avoided emissions are not yet available, but research work proceeds with the aim of deriving credible willingness to pay estimates to avoid the emissions in question.

As a result of the initiative Manweb has started similar (albeit larger) projects in the other regions: Crewe and Knowsley. For example, the Knowsley project aims to obtain cheap loans for energy-saving projects for about 400 small and medium-sized companies over the next three years under a £6 million DSM scheme financed by Manweb and the European Union. The aim is that the scheme should save 50 GWh of electricity and 36 000 tonnes of carbon dioxide per year.

Table 4.5   Environmental benefits of Manweb DSM programme

	CO_2	CH_4	N_2O	NO_2	CO	NMH_C	SO_2	Total
Emission factor (g/kWh)	936.8	3.50	0.05	4.55	0.14	0.02	6.03	
Value of avoided emissions (ECU/g)	–	–	–	–	–	–	-	
Annual savings (tonnes)								
year 1	–	–	–	–	–	–	–	
year 2	–	–	–	–	–	–	–	
year 3	–	–	–	–	–	–	–	
year 4	–	–	–	–	–	–	–	
year 5	–	–	–	–	–	–	–	
year 6	–	–	–	–	–	–	–	
Total savings (tonnes)								
Avoided externality	–	–	–	–	–	–	-	–
Net present value	–	–	–	–	–	–	-	–

The Energy Saving Trust's national promotion of CFLs to domestic customers

In the Conservative Party's Manifesto for the general election in April 1992 was a promise to establish an Energy Saving Trust (EST). The role of the EST is to introduce schemes to overcome the market barriers associated with improving the efficiency with which smaller consumers use energy. After its re-election, the Government had plans for the Energy Saving Trust to make a major contribution to its national programme for CO_2 reductions (that is, stabilization of CO_2 emissions at their 1990 level by 2000) (DOE, 1992). The government's commitment required introducing measures to reduce CO_2 emissions by 10 mtC (million tonnes of carbon) lower than they would otherwise have been, by 2000 (a 'reduction' of 6 per cent).[33] Indeed, the government gave the EST the specific task of achieving 25 per cent of the overall CO_2 reduction required to meet the stabilization objective.

It indicated that the Energy Saving Trust could be spending £400 million (ECU516 million) per annum within the next few years, funded by a 2–3 per cent levy on electricity and gas tariffs, to achieve this objective. The intention was that the regulators of the gas and electricity industries would allow such funding to be raised via levies on domestic consumers' gas and electricity bills. Both regulators decided, however, that it would be inappropriate for them to be responsible for raising such money. To date OFFER has allowed funding of some £100 million (ECU129 million) spread over four years, while OFGAS has refused to provide any money for programmes. As a result, the development of the EST has been constrained. Only a few pilot programmes are being operated while the burden of the organization's overheads are being carried by them.

Costs of CFL promotion   In October 1993 the Trust launched a pilot scheme to promote the sale of CFL in conjunction with lighting manufacturers, the Lighting Industry Federation and retailers (EST, 1994). It was sponsored by most of the regional electricity companies. Through working with these partners, the Trust was able to cut the cost of CFLs in participating shops by over one-third, from £15 to £10 (ECU19 to ECU13), resulting in a five-fold increase in sales. (Cheaper electromagnetic lamps – with worse power factor and harmonics – were also offered at a £1 discount: £5 (ECU6) instead of £6 (ECU8). Of this price reduction £4 was leveraged from the manufacturers and retailers, and most of the remaining cost was paid by the EST. During the eight-weeks of the scheme, about 740 000 CFL were sold, equal to the total sales of the same shops for the whole of 1992.[34] The EST has established that 42 per cent of those sold were electromagnetic lamps and 58 per cent were electronic lamps.

The campaign was supported with marketing material at point of sale in participating retailers. The onus for purchase and installation was left entirely to the consumer. Everyone was effectively eligible to benefit from the promotion. It has been estimated that the EST's additional costs of operating the programme (including general overheads) were approximately 10 per cent of the subsidy

Table 4.6 *Est DSM programme costs (ECU)*

Year	Penetration rate (%)	No. of CFL packs sold	Equipment cost Customer	Utility	Plus manu. ret. discount	Total	Customer Transaction	Installing/main.	Total customer costs	Utility Admin./overheads	Total utility cost	Society Misc.	Total programme costs
0	3.4	740 000	7 535 494	953 860	2 212 955	10 702 309	0	0	7 535 494	122 953	1 076 813	0	8 612 307

Table 4.7 *Est DSM programme benefits (ECU)*

Year	No. of participants	less free riders	add free drivers	Net participants	Annual electricity savings (MWh)	Private benefits Avoided costs (mECU/kWh)	Electricity cost savings	Avoided repurchases	Avoided transaction cost	Avoided main./disposal	Society Avoided cost (mECU/kWh)	Avoided electricity costs	Other avoided costs	Total avoided costs
0	740 000	113 846	0	626 154	63 993	11.92	7 627 770	564 979	0	0	3.70	2 367 374	564 979	2 932 353
1					63 993	11.92	7 627 770	564 979			3.70	2 367 374	564 979	2 932 353
2					63 993	11.92	7 627 770	1 129 958			3.70	2 367 374	1 129 958	3 497 331
3					63 993	11.92	7 627 770	564 979			3.70	2 367 374	564 979	2 932 353
4					63 993	11.92	7 627 770	1 129 958			3.70	2 367 374	1 129 958	3 497 331
5					30 682	11.92	3 657 150	0			3.70	1 135 042	0	1 135 042
Total					350 646		41 795 998	3 954 851	0	0		12 971 912	3 954 851	16 926 763
Present value							36 791 632	3 473 035				11 418 744	3 473 035	14 891 779

Notes: As table 4.3.

provided. As no follow-up evaluation was conducted there are no additional costs to be considered in later years. This gives a total programme cost of roughly ECU8.6 million (see Table 4.6).

Some information on the precise programme costs and benefits is regarded as confidential at this stage. As a result, in some cases informed estimates are provided.

Benefits of CFL promotion In terms of calculating programme benefits a number of problems arise because of the lack of detailed programme evaluation. The approximate number of free-riders can be established. The level of sales achieved in the eight-week campaign period was equal to the total sales generated in 1992. On this basis, it could be expected that in the absence of the campaign some 114 000 CFL would have been sold. This means that the campaign stimulated only 626 000 additional purchases.[35] In regard to free-drivers, there is no evidence to suggest that CFL sales (in non-participating stores) rose as a result of the programme. There is some evidence to suggest that sales of CFL were stimulated after the completion of the promotional period (according to the EST, due to awareness and so on). This appears to have increased sales by about 30 000 compared with the corresponding periods over the last two years. However, due to the uncertainty associated with this and with the number of free-riders, it has been decided to ignore this effect.

The EST undertook no comprehensive post-programme analysis to establish exactly what size bulb the CFL replaced, where they were put and hours of use. It also has no information regarding the quantity of each type of CFL sold. The manufacturers regard this as commercially confidential information. As a result, the energy-saving calculations should be viewed with caution; they are best estimates only.

These problems are to some extent overcome by making the following assumptions. The price of the CFL varies with wattage, so as we have assumed that all are the full-price variety we can also assume that all were 20W CFL replacing 100W GLS (on average). To take account of the likelihood that not all CFL will replace 100W incandescents, it has been assumed that the actual saving is not 80W but 70W. It has also been assumed that the average daily usage is some four hours (this is consistent with the work undertaken by Mills, 1993), and some initial research undertaken by the EST. This research (which does not claim to be representative) suggests that in 100W applications typical use is around 4–6 hours per day. The location affects the average daily hours of use, and although this does not affect the energy savings that accrue as a result of the programme, it does affect their timing, which in turn affects the net present value of the benefits. The promotional information stressed the need to ensure that CFL were placed in high-use locations.

On the basis of these assumptions and taking into account the societal avoided cost of electricity, the net present value of the avoided cost of the programme is approximately ECU15 million (see Table 4.7).

A guide to policies for energy conservation

Cost-effectiveness of CFL promotion   The cost-effectiveness of the programme
is illustrated in Table 4.8. It would indicate that on the basis of the assumptions
employed (which although conservative should be treated with some caution,
particularly in relation to avoided energy use) that the programme was clearly
cost-effective from society's viewpoint. Officials from the EST suggested that
a range of follow-on discount schemes would be planned, monitored and
evaluated more closely.

Table 4.8   Net present value of Energy Saving Trust's DSM programme

Costs and benefits (ECU)	
Total benefits	14 891 779
Total costs	8 612 307
Net present value	6 279 473
Benefit: cost ratio	1.7
Energy savings (ECU/kWh)	
DSM costs	2.5
Net saving	1.2
Cost-low	3.1
Cost-high	4.9
Capacity savings (ECU/kW)	
DSM costs	327
CCGT cost[a]	449

Note: [a]   CCGT = combined-cycle gas turbine.

Environmental benefits of CFL promotion   Table 4.9 shows the environmental
benefits of the programme. It assumes that coal is the marginal plant (as indeed
it generally is in the UK at the moment), although this may change for certain
periods of the year as more CCGT comes on line.

Table 4.9   Environmental benefits of the Energy Saving Trust's DSM programme

	CO_2	CH_4	N_2O	NO_2	CO	NMHC	SO_2	Total
Emission factor (g/kWh)	936.84	3.50	0.05	4.6	0.14	0.02	6.0	
Value of avoided emissions (mECU/g)	–	–	–	–	–	–	–	
Annual savings (tonnes)								
year 1	–	–	–	–	–	–		–
year 2	–	–	–	–	–	–		–
year 3	–	–	–	–	–	–		0.33

Table 4.9   (continued)

	CO_2	CH_4	N_2O	NO_2	CO	NMHC	SO_2	Total
year 4	–	–	–	–	–	–	–	
year 5	–	–	–	–	–	–	–	
year 6	–	–	–	–	–	–	–	
Total savings (tonnes)								
Avoided externality	–	–	–	–	–	–	–	–
Net present value	–	–	–	–	–	–	–	–

Note: Blanks are left in 'Value of avoided emissions' columns to signify that willingness to pay estimates are not yet available, but ongoing research is likely to yield some credible estimates of same for the future.

CONCLUSIONS AND RECOMMENDATIONS

• Drawing conclusions regarding the real costs and benefits of DSM as a *policy* instrument is extremely difficult. They depend very much on the approach adopted, a number of which are being tried. However, given the lack of experience in these matters it may be some time before the costs and benefits become fully apparent.

• It appears that an approach based on addressing the inherent disincentives which typical types of utility regulation generate would offer a relatively low-cost and robust way to proceed. This is because it would provide utilities with the appropriate incentives to pursue all the DSM that was in its interests, and would reward only successful efforts. As a result, less regulatory oversight, particularly in relation to monitoring and evaluation, would be necessary.

• Using DSM as a policy instrument, and creating a level playing field between demand and supply, need not involve substantial costs. In any case, these costs are likely to be reflected in the amount of cost-effective DSM identified.

• More work needs to be done on evaluating the real costs and benefits of DSM *programmes*. Analysing these costs and benefits is a difficult exercise, and the problem is exacerbated by the lack of consensus regarding which costs and benefits to include and by the difficulty in measuring some of them. It is clear that the costs and benefits of DSM vary considerably from programme to programme, because in essence the application of DSM is an exercise in marketing. This means that a multitude of options exist and that each should be considered on its merits, given the target market. It also suggests that an overly prescriptive approach, which may result in excessive regulatory oversight and limited flexibility, is less likely to be successful.

• There is considerable evidence to suggest that domestic lighting programmes *can* be cost-effective from society's viewpoint *before* accounting for environmental costs. Again, the variability in the costs and benefits of different programmes can, however, be very large.

• Given the high fixed cost of programmes, national programmes with substantial promotional support (perhaps at a local level through regional utilities) provide the most cost-effective opportunities for the promotion of efficient domestic lighting. It also encourages the full support of suppliers and retailers which is so essential to achieving high market penetration – the key to cost-effectiveness. The relatively long experience of the Dutch utilities in this regard offers perhaps the best example of domestic lighting programmes in practice. Although the objective of their efforts is environmental, a full cost-benefit analysis of the whole domestic lighting programme should be a priority.

APPENDIX: THE SOCIETAL AVOIDED COST OF UK ELECTRICITY

In order to develop a precise estimate of avoided cost for a DSM programme it would be necessary to model the workings of the electricity industry on a 'before and after' basis to see its effects precisely. Depending on the DSM employed, these avoided costs may vary to some degree (for example, a DSM which was saving primarily electricity at peak periods would have higher avoided costs than one that was saving off-peak electricity). Because of this complexity general figures reflecting the typical avoidable costs are usually the most sensible way to undertake such an analysis.

According to OFFER (1994b), the final price of electricity for customers as a whole is broken down as follows: generation 56 per cent, distribution 24 per cent, transmission 5 per cent, supply 5 per cent and the fossil fuel levy nearly 10 per cent. In its report for the regulator, SRC provided estimates of the benefits of DSM programmes in the UK (see LE Energy Ltd and SRC International ApS, 1992). It uses as a base case an avoided cost of electricity generation of 2.5 pence/kWh (ECU0.032/kWh), and then adds 0.37 pence/kWh (ECU0.005/kWh) for avoided transmission and distribution costs.[36] This gives a total avoided cost of 2.87 pence/kWh (ECU0.037/kWh). This is the figure used in the analysis for the programmes in this report (see Tables 4.3 and 4.7). It acknowledges that the avoidance of transmission and distribution costs is, however, unlikely to be smooth.

These estimates appear to be reasonable. OFFER (1993a) recently concluded that the short-run avoidable costs of National Power and PowerGen are 2.82 pence/kWh (ECU0.036/kWh) and 2.73 pence/kWh (ECU0.035/kWh) respectively. This includes the coal premium (without which the figures would be 2.52 pence and 2.55 pence (ECU0.032 and ECU0.033) respectively). The Director General of Electricity Supply 'capped' the pool after a series of investigations into unanticipated price increases. The caps are for an average annual pool purchase price of 2.4 pence/kWh (ECU0.031/kWh) time weighted and 2.55 pence/kWh (ECU0.033/kWh) demand weighted (in October 1993 prices) (OFFER, 1994a). Actual prices had been in excess of these figures. By comparison, the International Energy Agency estimates that the cost of electricity from new CCGT is between 2.4 and 3.7 pence/kWh (ECU0.031 and ECU0.048/kWh), depending on gas prices.[37]

NOTES

1. LE Energy Ltd and SRC International ApS (1992, p. 2). This was the definition used in the context of the study.
2. The sole test in relation to DSM is whether the economic benefits outweigh the economic costs. It includes transferring demand from periods of higher electricity prices to periods when prices are lower. Whilst this overlaps traditional load management the tools used may be wider than load shifting (that is, using strategic energy conservation). Although this chapter focuses on electricity, DSM could also be used by gas utilities and transport systems.
3. To the extent that these are overcoming what are considered to be disincentives in a 'market' created by imperfect regulation, it may be harsh to describe them as costs. There are, however, real costs associated with introducing change and, as perfect regulation does not exist, at the margin cost-benefit analysis may be the most practical alternative.
4. See California Public Utilities Commission, Decision 93-09-078 (17 September 1993).
5. All monetary figures have also been given in ECU using a mid-December 1994 commercial exchange rate: ECU1 = £0.7758 = US$1.2125 = Dkr 7.471 = Fl 2.133 = DM 1.9045. However, where information has been taken directly from previous research, the exchange rate at the time the research was undertaken has been used.
6. In other words, ensuring that the price controls are truly cost-reflective so that the way a utility earns its revenues is directly related to the underlying cost structures.
7. The price controls do not limit the RECs' profits directly, but rather the unit prices they can charge. 'RPI-X' limits the increases in the prices the RECs can charge between price control reviews.
8. In the United States the cost-effectiveness of utility-sponsored programmes is evaluated using the 'Standard Practice Methodology for Economic Analysis of DSM Programs' developed by the California Energy Commission and the California Public Utility Commission, San Francisco, October 1987.
9. The claim is made on the basis that an independent energy efficiency supplier would have to cover these costs.
10. Related to this may be any increase in energy consumption associated with the general expenditure of the additional disposable income, and the effect of the marginal increase in the price of electricity to all consumers (if that is how DSM is funded) on energy consumption, although often in North America the latter is regarded as a transfer payment. Analysing these costs would require looking at the price and income elasticity of energy demand.

11. This is because for tariff-paying customers the sunk (avoidable) costs of electricity are collected in a unit charge.

12. Derived from F. Fichtner for the European Commission (DGXVII), *The Potential for Energy Saving in the Applications of Electrical Energy*, Stuttgart, June 1988. These are rough estimates only, particularly in relation to the tertiary sector.

13. Most of the programmes identified by Mills have operated in Sweden, Denmark and, to a lesser extent, the Netherlands.

14. Letter from Eckhard Schulz, VDEW, Frankfurt, 13 July, 1994.

15. Prof. Peter Hennicke, Wuppertal Institute, June 1994.

16. Dr Willi Herbert, private communication, September 1994.

17. The Dutch government has set itself the objective of stabilizing carbon dioxide emissions at their 1990 level by 1995 and achieving significant reductions beyond that date. A further objective is to stabilize overall energy demand by 2000. It is estimated that these objectives will require a variety of policy initiatives, including an increase in the annual rate of energy efficiency improvement to over 2 per cent per annum. This would match the country's achievements during the period 1973–85, but would be very much faster than the 0.5–1 per cent per annum rate recorded in more recent years.

18. Their part of the plan is summarized in the Dutch Energy Distribution Sector Steering Committee, *Environmental Action Plan of the Energy Distribution Sector in the Netherlands*, Apeldoorn, 1991.

19. Samenwerkende Elektriciteits Produktiebedrijven (SEP) is a limited liability company wholly owned by the generators and is essentially the middle man, playing the key operational and planning role for the industry. It is currently undertaking a least-cost planning pilot study under the SAVE programme, the objective of which is to identify the cost-effective potential for DSM.

20. Letter from Peter Nieuwenhuyse of EnergieNed, Arnhem, 21 July 1994.

21. Private communication with EnergieNed, September 1994. This equals Fl2.35 per CFL.

22. Private communication with EBA, September 1994. The costs of the programme include customer costs of Fl18.95 (ECU8.9) (no subsidy was offered), and the cost of personnel, material and external costs of Fl168,361 (ECU78,932).

23. Maintaining this reduction would allow this costly option to be deferred for another five years; see Electricity UK, 'Island aims for big power savings', *Electricity Association*, no. 13, April 1993, p. 6.

24. In the commercial sector low-energy lights (PLEC lamps) and hot-water cylinder insulation schemes are also of some importance. In addition, free energy audits and energy-efficiency advice was provided, with concentration on the area of refrigeration. In the industrial sector attempts have been made to encourage the use of high-efficiency motors, improvements to compressed air systems to stop compressors working unnecessarily, additional metering to allow close correlation of electricity use with output, encouraging the company to manage its energy use more carefully, and power factor correction equipment to adjust the precise delivery of electric current to the specific needs of the site.

25. The Manweb shop (showroom) in Holyhead town centre is one of the focal points of the campaign. Another is the nearby office of the Holyhead Opportunities Trust, which deals with all the applications for low-energy lamps, lagging jackets, insulation and draught-proofing and gives energy advice. The charity-based organization was established to help the regeneration of Holyhead economically, socially and environmentally, and this includes retraining the unemployed. The Welsh Development Agency helped with the setting-up and early funding of the organization, which now relies on projects such as Manweb's to help it continue. Local authorities are also enthusiastic supporters of the project. Mercury communications has donated a telephone advice line which residents can use free, and Philips has provided low-energy lamps at a discount. Local retailers apart from Manweb have joined in the promotion of low-energy lamps and appliances, and can qualify for the cash-rebate scheme when selling approved products to their customers.

26. Private communication with Manweb official, August 1994.

27. It is also assumed that there is no interaction between the use of CFL and any changes in the heating and cooling requirements of the house. *Ceteris paribus* one would expect that the heating requirement of the participating households would have increased marginally as a result of

the use of CFL. The cooling requirement should also have fallen, although natural ventilation is the predominant form of cooling in UK dwellings.

28. As the programme is asking the consumer to replace the GLS with a CFL possibly before the end of its natural life – presumably to be moved into a lower lighting use area – it is assumed that the replaced GLS had a full lifetime's operation left. The number of replacement purchases is therefore seven.

29. The other key criticism on the cost side is the poor accounting for utility overhead costs.

30. Private discussions with Manweb officials, September 1994.

31. The EU subsidy was £80 000 compared with the total estimated Holyhead project cost of £500 000. The EU subsidy costs relevant to the lighting programme have been included in the utility costs.

32. The difference between a (kilovolt ampere) and a kilowatt depends upon a power factor. The kVA is the apparent or total power and kW is the true power. The power factor is the percentage of current in an alternating-current circuit which is used as energy for the intended need. It is the ratio of useful power in watts to the apparent power taken by the load, and is usually below unity because the current and voltage are not in phase.

33. In the UK savings in CO_2 are generally referred to in million tonnes of carbon, not million tonnes of carbon dioxide.

34. According to the Trust, this scheme should continue to save electricity well beyond the lifetime of the CFLs purchased, as consumers are more likely to repeat buy rather than revert to conventional bulbs. In addition, resulting publicity should raise the overall level of awareness of energy-saving lighting, leading to increased general use. Evidence to suggest this was available.

35. This excludes any possible seasonal sales effect which could vary this estimate, although in all likelihood not by much.

36. The second figure is calculated on the basis that typical domestic lighting programmes have a benefit: cost ratio of 1.94:1 when generation costs alone are considered (at 2.5 pence/kWh), and a benefit: cost ratio of 2.23:1 when transmission and distribution benefits are allowed for.

37. This equates to 3.72 and 5.88 US cents/kWh in 1992 prices, using current exchange rates (£1:$1.58), and a 10 per cent discount rate. The investment cost is £600/kW. See IEA, *Electricity Supply in the OECD*, Paris, 1992.

REFERENCES

Association for the Conservation of Energy (ACE) (1993), *Electricity for the Future: A Response to OFFER'S Consultation Document on the Review of the Distribution Price Control*, London: ACE.

Department of the Environment (DoE) (1992), *Climate Change: Our National Programme for CO_2 Emissions*, London: DoE.

Electric Power Research Institute (EPRI) (1993), *Drivers of Electricity Growth and the Role of Utility Demand-Side Management*, Palo Alto, CA: EPRI.

EnergieNed (1994), *Resultaten Nationale Spaarlampenactie 1993/4: Milieu Aktie Plan Energiedistributiesector*, Arnhem: EnergieNed.

Energy Saving Trust (1994), *Factsheet Number Four*, London: Energy Saving Trust.

International Energy Agency (IEA) (1989), *Electricity End-use Efficiency*, Paris: IEA.

International Energy Agency (IEA) (1992), *Electricity Supply in the OECD*, Paris: IEA.

Joskow, Paul L. (1994), 'More from the guru of energy efficiency: "There must be a pony"', *Electricity Journal*, 7(4).

LE Energy Ltd and SRC International ApS (1992), *Demand-side Measures*, Birmingham: Office of Electricity Regulation.

Lovins, Amory B. (1994), 'Apples, oranges and horned toads: is the Joskow and Marron critique of electric efficiency costs valid?', *Electricity Journal*, **7**(4).

Manweb (1993a), *Energy Efficiency Power Saved Project*, Briefing Note, Chester: Manweb.

Manweb (1993b), *Power Save Holyhead Project*, Chester: Manweb.

Manweb (1994), *Final Report for the European Commission on the Holyhead Power Save Project*, Chester: Manweb.

Mills, Evan (1991a), 'Evaluation of European lighting programmes: utilities finance energy efficiency', *Energy Policy*, **19**(3), 266–78.

Mills, Evan (1991b), 'Using financial incentives to promote compact fluorescent lamps in Europe: cost effectiveness and consumer response in ten countries', in *Proceedings of the 1st European Conference on Energy-efficient Lighting*, Stockholm, 29–30 May.

Mills, Evan (1993), 'Efficient lighting programmes in Europe: cost effectiveness, consumer response, and market dynamics', *Energy: The International Journal*, **18**(2), 75–98.

Ministry of Economic Affairs (The Netherlands) (1990), *Memorandum on Energy Conservation*, The Hague: Ministry of Economic Affairs.

Morovic, Tihomir (1993), 'The VEBA contract: a new form of co-operation between government and an electric utility', in *The Energy Efficiency Challenge for Europe*, ECEEE Proceedings, vol. 1, Rungstedgård: ECEEE.

Oak Ridge National Laboratory (1989), *The Administrative Costs of Energy Conservation Programmes*, Oak Ridge, Tennessee: Oak Ridge National Laboratory.

Office of Electricity Regulation (OFFER) (1992), *Regulator Tightens Control on National Grid Company Prices*, Birmingham: OFFER.

Office of Electricity Regulation (OFFER) (1993a), *Pool Price Statement*, Birmingham: OFFER.

Office of Electricity Regulation (OFFER) (1993b), *The Supply Price Control: Proposals*, Birmingham: OFFER.

Office of Electricity Regulation (OFFER) (1994a), *Decision on a Monopolies and Mergers Commission Reference*, Birmingham: OFFER.

Office of Electricity Regulation (OFFER) (1994b),*The Distribution Price Control Proposals*, Birmingham: OFFER.

Wilms, Wim and Evan Mills (1993), 'Analysis of price and non-price factors influencing the adoption of compact fluorescent lamps by European households', in *Proceedings of the 2nd European Conference on Energy Efficiency Lighting*, Arnhem, 26-29 September.

5. Institutional design: area implementation of energy conservation in France

A. Bonduelle, Michel Colombier, P. Radanne and Kenya Tillerson

INTRODUCTION

In the analysis of policies for energy conservation institutional issues have been somewhat neglected. Yet, when one European country is compared with another, certain invariable factors appear, such as the establishment, in most countries, of public organizations charged with the implementation of energy efficiency policies. But notable differences also occur between the scope of the missions of these organizations (from research to development), the financial mechanisms (directly by the State or through contracts), their level of dependence on central administration, and finally, the level of attention given to the decentralization of policies, whose origin can be essentially found in each country's tradition, but also in its size: it is clear that the question of decentralization is not addressed in the same way in Germany, France, Ireland and the Netherlands.

This diversity is the result of the large differences between the organization of energy sectors on one hand and the institutional structure of each country on the other, and is reflected in the implementation of local policies. In some countries, the implementation of energy efficiency policies is directly implemented by local authorities; in others this role is played, to a large extent, by the energy utilities, national public agencies or decentralized ministerial services.

Experience has shown that the modes of organization can be just as significant for the success of demand-orientated policies as they are for supply-orientated ones (the respective role of the public and private sectors, the level of centralization and so on). But no comparative analysis of these organizational modes has been undertaken, such as that carried out for the electricity production and distribution sector.

Our objective here is to take France as a case study for which we had easy access to information and data. France has experienced a progressive evolution in energy efficiency policies since 1974: at an institutional level, with the progressive implementation of regional structures aimed at implementing national policies and with the development of regional governments since the strengthening of their authority in 1981 and 1982.

Specifically, our objective is to analyse the contribution of regional teams to the implementation of energy efficiency policies. The issue of efficiency will be addressed here through the link established between the initial objectives, their territorial implementation and their actual results.

We will analyse the role played by a team acting at a regional level, charged with the implementation of concrete projects and equipped with the necessary means and scope of action to elaborate a strategy.

To this end, we have chosen two approaches :

- the first is quantitative and makes an assessment of the various successive systems of public aid to conservation investment. It attempts to link the heterogeneous impacts of these systems with the institutional modalities which characterize their implementation. In theory, we possess an almost perfect experimental frame: a 'same tool' public aid to investment, with different applications for the potential beneficiaries according to the period. In practice, the analysis is confused by other variables with a strong impact on these policies, most notably the decrease in energy prices since the mid-1980s;
- the second is qualitative and attempts to describe in a hierarchical manner the tasks regional teams can carry out in their field of action. These teams should not be analysed as an independent instrument, but as a place where instruments can be implemented in a co-ordinated manner, according to strategic objectives.

Before undertaking this analysis, a historical overview of the context of energy management policy implementation in France is presented.

ENERGY POLICY CONTEXT IN FRANCE

A Supply-side Response to the First Oil Crisis

The response to the first oil crisis of 1973 mainly consisted in increasing national energy output as well as nuclear programmes (often considered safer at the time because less dependent on raw material importation). Nevertheless, an energy conservation policy was initiated in France immediately following the oil shock. The Agency for Energy Savings (AEE) was established in 1974. However, the lack of specialized experts proved to be a strong barrier to the development of an energy efficiency policy.

The investigation of potential energy savings, the progressive improvement of equipment, the elaboration of energy auditing methodologies and expert training were gradually undertaken, although they were not immediately integrated into public programmes. The response to the first oil crisis in the mid-1970s was essentially a state initiative.

A Demand-side Response to the Second Oil Crisis

This situation changed significantly during the second oil crisis in 1979. In six years a professional network had emerged, armed with the efficient methods and equipment which had become available. Thus, a demand-side response became possible.

The energy efficiency policies developing at European level found strong support in the nation states as well as the territorial authorities (regions and municipalities) because of the urgent need to reduce oil dependence. Simultaneously, the high prices of hydrocarbons stimulated the market for conservation. Training professionals and decision-makers in the new approaches to energy management was no longer an obstacle. Programmes were, therefore, developed and became extensive after the second oil crisis. European energy efficiency policies were very diverse, reflecting the multitude of institutional structures. Their motivation and level of engagement varied depending on whether they were implemented by the state, the regions or the municipalities. The more decentralized a country's structure, the more, under strong pressure from public opinion, energy efficiency policies were supplied with substantial means.

A complete reversal of the post-war tendency took place. Until then, those countries which had nationalized their energy systems were seen as 'models' because of their strong policies. The implementation of the new energy efficiency policies based on the consumers' interests was focused more on the mobilization of market mechanisms. Their dynamism mainly consisted in the link established between consumers, professionals and territorial authorities. Therefore, the countries operating decentralised energy policies (Denmark, Germany, the Netherlands) became the new 'models'.

The Crisis for Energy Conservation Policies Following the Third Oil Shock

The progress of energy efficiency policies was interrupted in 1985 during the oil counter-shock and the return of prices, in real terms, to their 1973 level. However, a second factor, just as important, should be considered: the financial crisis of the states. Confronted with financial deficits in social programmes and rising unemployment, they discontinued subsidizing industrial policies as social aid expenses increase. They looked to the market to take the place of public intervention.

It is now possible to draw conclusions on this issue. The market on its own did not become the mechanism for conservation and progress towards improved energy efficiency and local energy resources is delayed throughout the whole of Europe. This situation illustrates the weakness of energy efficiency policies when the sense of crisis disappears.

OVERVIEW OF ENERGY MANAGEMENT POLICIES

Regulatory Policies

We will refer to two examples of regulatory actions implemented in France after the first oil crisis: thermal regulations in new buildings and the inspection of large energy consuming enterprises. The conclusions that can be reached from the viewpoint of a local team are quite different.

Thermal regulations in new buildings
The aims of thermal regulations in new buildings are three-fold:

1. to make the insulation of buildings mandatory (the factor G characterizes the level of efficiency);
2. to create a market for efficient space-heating systems. In fact, regulation favours electric heating (low investment) and natural gas;
3. to lead to a stronger industrialization of the building sector and improved organization of building sites.

Contrary to other countries, the standards introduced in France concerned overall efficiency and not any particular means to this end. It is therefore up to the relevant operator to choose between alternatives in order to reach the required efficiency level, that is, by insulating or improving generator efficiency.

The state has repeatedly made the standards stricter: in 1974, it established the first thermal regulation, and this was reinforced for space-heating in 1977. In 1982, a new law was passed. In 1985, a large demonstration operation programme preceded the 1989 legislation now in application. The implementation of these regulations was characterized by:

- *inclusiveness*: the legislators were particularly keen to associate the entire construction sector in a collective effort because they were aware that introducing innovative techniques would constitute, in the beginning, a handicap for artisans and small firms;

- *no price increase*: the increase in energy efficiency was obtained without a rise in prices of dwellings. The introduction of standards made massive dissemination possible with improvements in construction techniques and the drop in materials prices;
- *durability*: after 20 years of application, this legislation illustrates the advantages of stability in the choices made;
- *administrative homogeneity*: the Departmental Directorates for Equipment representing the Ministry of Housing applied the regulations uniformly over the entire territory. In fact, until 1982, these administrations were responsible for issuing building permits in France (currently, the municipalities have this responsibility).

Along with these undeniable advances, there were also some shortcomings: the thermal regulation favoured electric heating and disregarded the issue of renewable sources of energy. Property developers favoured the least expensive heating systems without considering their energy efficiency. The legislation thus improved construction methods but not thermal installations. A lack of involvement of the local authorities in enforcing the legislation as a consequence of the centralized character of the procedure was evident. This resulted in a lack of transfer of know-how and capacity to control the application to the services which are now in charge of issuing building permits.

To conclude, the use of the state's legislative authority is an effective tool for achieving dissemination of energy efficiency and to decrease the unit price of the elements which go into energy conservation. However, the lack of on-site follow-up leads to a great deal of non-compliance.

The inspection of installations consuming more than 300 TOE per year
In July 1977, a decree made mandatory the regular inspection of thermal installations which consume more than 300 tonnes of oil equivalent (TOE) per year. This regulation primarily concerns industrial firms but also includes large service and commercial sector facilities (hospitals, district heating boilers, and so on). These audits, carried out every three years by inspection bodies (such as the Apaves and Veritas), aim to advise these establishments on technical improvements.

At first, this regulation achieved its objective of identifying opportunities. However, quite rapidly, because the technical culture concerning energy savings had spread in large firms, the audit requirement became nothing more than a formality which had no real effect on the decisions made (the periodic audit does not correspond to the real terms of decision-making; the inspection bodies standardize their analysis, which thus loses any concrete effectiveness, and so on).

The bureaucratic application of these procedures became an obstacle in itself. The administration prevents the results of the audits being used in the development of regional programmes (for reasons regarding the secrecy of statistics). This legislation is still in force and generates expense for firms and the administration but without achieving any results.

The Institutional Policies

Immediately after the first oil crisis, in 1974 France established a national organization charged with implementing the policy on the rational use of energy defined by the government: the Agency for Energy Savings (AEE). In conformity with French administrative tradition, the AEE was a centralized organization under the authority of the Ministry of Industry, which provided the finance. The regional structure consisted of only a few engineers in the Regional Directorates for Industry and Research (DRIRE) which are the regional services of the Ministry. In this context, the Agency's activities mainly consisted of training and communication, the preparation of regulations, and the evaluation of projects submitted for financing in the frame of simple standard procedures (see below).

In 1982, an important development took place: the creation of the French Agency for Energy Management (AFME), which combined the AEE with two other existing organizations, the Commissariat for Solar Energy (COMES) and the District Heating Mission (charged with the development of district heating in France) under the Ministry of Industry. The scope of technical competence of the new Agency was thus enlarged to include renewable energies. However, two other factors are of greater importance:

1. the extension of its scope of action to include research and development (the Agency worked under the joint responsibility of the Ministry of Industry and the Ministry of Research) ;
2. the decentralization of its organization. Indeed, the creation of the AFME came within the framework of the administrative decentralization dynamic launched in 1981 which reinforced the territorial authorities, in particular the regional governments. AFME was thus equipped with 26 regional delegations, each with a staff of 10–20, within the regional structure and located in each French region. These teams are backed by the national office (for training, communication, economic studies, technical support) and serve as relays for the implementation of financial aid procedures. Most importantly, they receive regionalized budgets which permit them to develop partnerships with regional actors.

The AFME developed a policy of partnership with regional governments which led to contracts (*contrats de plan*) programming the implementation of regional energy management funds (FRMEs), funded jointly by the AFME (representing the state) and the regions. These contracts aim to finance regional policy actions. With the exception of Rhône-Alpes and Nord-Pas de Calais regions, which had autonomously developed regional agencies and where the competencies are shared, the regional delegations of the AFME are, as a rule, the technical teams charged with the preparation and *ex ante* evaluation of the FRME projects.

The latest development dates from 1992, with the creation of Ademe (Agency for the Environment and Energy Management) which combined the AFME, ANRED (National Agency for Waste Recuperation) and AQA (Air Quality Agency). The organizational scheme of AFME was maintained (ANRED and AQA were centralized agencies comparable to the former AEE) and the scope of intervention broadened to include waste, air quality and noise pollution.

The Financial Aids to Investment for the Rational Use of Energy

The 400 francs per TOE procedure
It took close to four years, from 1974 to 1978, for the AEE to build up its team and develop intervention methods. The question its executives addressed is: How to disseminate energy conservation as quickly as possible in the various activity sectors?

The Agency had hardly any regional relays: a few engineers in the Regional Directorates for Industry and Research (DRIRE) in each region represented the Ministry of Industry. It was therefore impossible to carry out detailed technical project analysis due to the lack of staff. Given the urgency of the situation, Jean Sirota, the Director General of the Agency, proposed a simple system: a fixed bonus per TOE saved regardless of the sector or the project. The AEE's Paris office was in charge of evaluating the largest projects submitted, essentially the industrial ones. The DRIRE engineers were in charge of smaller projects. Often, because of a lack of experts, the projects were handed over to installers for evaluation. This procedure remained in force from 1978 to 1980.

The Special Fund for Large Operations (FSGT)
This programme was implemented from 1982 to 1987 and financed by an additional tax on automobile fuel. It was discontinued after the combined decreases in the price of oil and the value of the dollar.

Here again, along with clearly energy-related objectives, other objectives intervene in the implementation modalities: to respond to the second oil crisis by boosting energy savings and substitution investments; to boost the activity of the building sector by promoting conservation-related construction; to disseminate energy savings in new activity sectors (public administration, notably the local authorities, hospitals and small and medium-sized enterprises (SMEs), and so on).

The institutional context of this fund differs from that of the 400 francs per TOE programme. The AFME, formerly the AEE, set up regional delegations. This led to individual approaches to the evaluation procedures for the projects submitted, all with a similar objective: to make massive energy savings.

The Regional Funds for Energy Management (FRMEs)

The FRMEs were set up in 1983 with equal co-financing from AFME and the regional governments. Decisions are made by a joint management committee.

Investigation procedures vary by region and over time, but nevertheless possess certain common characteristics. These subsidies are not orientated towards investment aids (with the exception of local communities); the subsidy for each case is negotiated – there is no standard rate; priority is given to restructuring regional industries (renewable energies, economic sectors strongly established in the region, and so on).

In recent years, some of these subsidies have been discontinued because of the reduced level of investment being supported by the regional councils. Furthermore, the reduction of AFME's budget resulted in the reduction of the regional budgets. In addition to these three programmes, other subsidies have been allocated over the past 20 years. They concern essentially studies and demonstrations.

THE IMPLEMENTATION OF PUBLIC SUBSIDIES AND THE INSTITUTIONAL CONTEXT IN FRANCE, 1975–92

Confronted with the oil shocks, all the European states took measures to reduce their dependence on imported oil and to limit the risk to their economy. Most of them introduced legislation and standards, promoted technical exchange and research and implemented fiscal measures to promote efficient uses of energy. Some countries also invested in gas, electricity or coal production.

However, as well as these traditional activities of the public authorities, we will address here the direct subsidies to energy consumers that France provided between 1973 and 1988. The subsidies amounted to some FFr7 billion (more than ECU1 billion) and the induced investments FFr37.5 billion (ECU5.7 billion). The use to which these substantial sums were put will be the object of this analysis.

In addition to the financial aids evaluated here, other instruments and policies were implemented, such as research support, consolidation of technical professional centres and better information. For instance, to support conservation in small enterprises, a 50 per cent subsidy (and sometimes more) was provided for energy studies and audits. In the commercial and service sector, new thermal regulations and improved consumer awareness led to a significant decrease in consumption in new or existing buildings. The progress made in building insulation, combined with improvements in boilers, resulted in a 70 per cent decrease in consumption in new dwellings between 1973 and 1990. A similar result is far from being obtained in public and service sector buildings.

The estimated figures were obtained by calculating the return on more than 20 000 implemented projects. This evaluation takes into account energy prices over the period studied, inflation and the operating lifetime of the projects carefully calculated. The data came from Ademe's energy accounts in 13 of the 28 French regions, representing close to 60 per cent of France's economy. This representative sample covers all branches of the economy and all types of technologies, and can therefore be extrapolated to the whole of France.

We first present a global analysis of the method and the results, then a differentiation of three aid systems.

The Sectoral Results

After the oil shocks in the 1970s, France launched strong voluntary public policies to reduce its dependence on imported energies. Although frequent mention is made of the French nuclear programme, the fact must not be overlooked that energy efficiency programmes developed in France are among the most important in Europe, in terms of both the sums invested and the establishment of specialized teams.

In the industrial sector, oil consumption (including petrol) was 24.1 MTOE[1] in 1973. In 1990, it was divided by a factor of 2.6, dropping to 9.2 MTOE. This reflects the achievements of the energy independence and energy efficiency policies in this sector. The improvement in regard to energy intensity is even more significant since, over the same period, industrial production increased by 30 per cent.

Part of the decrease observed is, however, the result of the economic crisis, during which, in the early 1980s, there were negative growth rates in all the European Union countries (activity effect). The decline of heavy industry, a large energy consumer, as well as the tendency to delocalize outside of Europe which also had an impact on the consumption figures above (structural effect). Finally, substantial gains were made due to energy savings and improvements in the efficiency of various procedures (the improvement of energy intensity in industrial production).

The most significant advances in France were made in the agricultural and food sector, especially in the sugar industry, and in the paper and cardboard sector, notably in terms of waste recovery and the use of 'waste' wood. In these sectors, concern for both the environment and energy savings combined. In other industries, the introduction of efficient technologies for drying, evaporation or mechanical vapour recompression fall under a much wider frame of modernization where energy is only one criterion among others. Finally, combined heat and power was only a limited success during the period studied although its development has since gained momentum.

In the domestic and service sector, in spite of important efforts in insulation and in the improvement of the heating systems, global consumption stabilized over the 1973–92 period. This situation results from two phenomena: the increase in the number or size of dwellings/offices, and so on; enhancement of the equipment of households, both in space heating (installation of central heating in old dwellings) and domestic appliances. Oil consumption has decreased and coal consumption almost disappeared, while gas (+171 per cent) and electricity (+220 per cent) have increased.

The energy-saving and substitution operations undertaken in social housing, hospitals, vacation facilities, swimming pools, communal buildings and public lighting have helped efficient technologies to penetrate the market and, moreover, have furthered energy management practices in these sectors. There remains, however, much to do in state buildings, in refrigeration installations and in lighting.

Overall, in transportation, energy management policies have failed. The effects of individual equipment improvements have not compensated sufficiently for the explosion in road transportation (+60 per cent between 1973 and 1990). The overall energy consumption of transportation increased 39.4 per cent between 1973 and 1990, from 32.5 MTOE to 45.3 MTOE. This 2 per cent average annual increase is twice the growth rate of final energy, which is 1 per cent over the same period.

The element which most determines consumption by transportation is not the 'number effect' nor the rate of equipment but the use which is made of vehicles. The average home–job distance has almost doubled over the period; also, the transportation of heavy goods has been replaced by numerous deliveries of small quantities linked to the structure of industry and its 'just-in-time' requirements. Finally, road transportation has few attractive alternatives unlike oil used in the household or in industry.

How to Evaluate these Policies

The examples of public aid studied here represent the majority of subsidized projects undertaken in the last 20 years in France. In industry, public action was massive: 1992 ECU0.55 billion were provided in subsidies. They triggered, between 1975 and 1992, ECU2.1 billion in energy management investments.

In the domestic and service sector, ECU0.43 billion in subsidies led to ECU1.65 billions in investments. An estimated ECU1.54 million in direct aid led to ECU8 million in investments in transportation being allocated in a regional context.

We will study the impact of these investments on consumer expenses and, more globally, on the economy. Once these data have been collected, we will calculate the return on investment, amortization periods and rent effects. We will then observe the methodological limits of the calculations and discuss the other positive impacts of public aid on investment policies.

Available data
Essentially, this analysis is based on the database compiled by the Agency for Energy Savings (AEE) between 1974 and 1981, and by the AFME from 1982 to 1993 in 13 regions. We only analyse subsidized investment operations. For these subsidized operations, a computer database exists which provides sufficient data: 4709 industrial operations, 13 749 in the domestic and service sector, 91 in agriculture, only 37 in transportation. Of these operations analysed, 2320 occur in the first period of direct national aids to energy savings, 15 057 comprise the aids to investment allocated by the regional delegations of the AFME, and 1848 come from the regional funds (FRMEs) administered jointly by the state and the regions.

This detailed knowledge comes from the data held in 13 of the 28 French regions by the Enercompta program and database, developed in 1988 by INESTENE for the regional delegations of AFME. It indexes the energy management operations subsidized by the AEE, then the AFME, since 1974 and the operations carried out with the regional governments within the framwork of the FRMEs.

The savings and substitutions in the regions concerned were first related to oil: 2.94 MTOE saved yearly, that is, 7.2 per cent of consumption. A total of 0.77 MTOE of coal was introduced into industry, while 0.396 MTOE of gas was saved, 0.256 MTOE substituted and 0.178 MTOE introduced into industry and the domestic and service sector. Other operations concern the sale of heat and renewable energies such as wood or waste.

The regions which used Enercompta represent approximately 60 per cent of the gross domestic product of France: Alsace, Aquitaine, Bourgogne, Bretagne, Champagne-Ardenne, Centre, Franche-Comté, Haute Normandie, Languedoc-Roussillon, Limousin, Nord-Pas de Calais, Poitou-Charente, Rhône-Alpes. To obtain results at the national level, we weighted the results of these regions according to their respective shares in the main branches of economy.[2]

Each investment is described in a computer file which provides three types of information:

- a physical description of the investment (for instance, type of boiler, energy used, quantity of energy consumed before and after the operation);
- energy data: the energy flow is divided into savings and substitutions. These data were entered during the evaluation of the projects. When up-dates or later evaluations are made, this new information is taken into account;
- financial data: the cost of the investment, amount of the subsidy, the reduction in expenses induced by the energy savings or the substitution, the pay-back period.

Reduction of expenses and profitability of the investment

To evaluate the impact of the operations for the actors, several assumptions have been made:

- *the investment pay-back periods* estimated initially were often based on risky projections; we now use actual energy prices in making our profitability rate calculations;
- *the lifetime of the equipment* has been estimated at 15 years for a boiler, 30 years for building insulation. Beyond this lifetime, it is assumed that the investment ceases to provide savings, which necessitates the extremely unfavourable hypothesis of returning to the low-efficiency equipment used previously;
- *the obsolescence rate* reflects the deterioration in performance over time and thus a decrease in the savings made. This rate measures the wear of the equipment. It is applied from the fourth year and is 5 per cent per annum during the lifetime of the investment in industry and 3 per cent per annum in the domestic and service sectors;
- *the price of energy sources*: the actual prices were taken into account from the evaluation period onward to follow the evolution of prices of various energies by the consumer sector. This was calculated both for saved and substituted energy sources.[3]
- *inflation*: the calculations take actual inflation into account. The inflation and interest rate trends were clearly a disadvantage for investors over the period (decrease in inflation, increase in interest rates in real terms).

These assumptions allow us to calculate the reduction in expenses according to the flows in energy, and the energy savings according to the price of these energies. These data are presented either in current ECU, 1992 ECU or dicounted 1992 ECU (at the 8 per cent rate used in France by the administration). The financial information contained in each file allows us to calculate an amortization which corresponds to the cumulated reduction of expenses over the amount of the investment minus the subsidy. This reduction takes into account, when possible, the other operating gains or expenses (more staff, less maintenance,

Table 5.1 Decrease in consumer expenses (ECU10^9) for the 13 regions studied

Year	Annual deflated value	Annual actualized deflated value	Cumulated actualized deflated value	Energy efficiency income after investment repayment	Energy efficiency income from the point of view of the operators (added subsidies)
1975	−0.15	−0.46	−0.46	−38.62	−28.62
1977	−23.08	−80.46	−103.38	−1 040.62	−907.69
1979	−204.77	−605.54	−996.31	−1 799.69	−1 416.31
1981	−581.23	−1 454.46	−3 614.46	−199.23	303.23
1983	−755.08	−1 599.23	−6 852.15	2 186.92	2 872.15
1985	−720.15	−1 290.92	−9 911.23	3 510.15	4 578.77
1987	−420.15	−637.54	−11 387.08	4 173.38	5 436.92
1989	−471.23	−605.08	−12 518.77	5 246.92	6 519.08
1991	−553.54	−601.69	−13 830.15	6 527.69	7 804.62
1993	−419.85	−387.69	−14 730.92	7 428.62	8 705.54
1995	−328.46	−255.69	−15 336.15	8 033.69	9 310.62
1997	−261.08	−172.00	−15 732.00	8 429.54	9 706.46
1999	−219.69	−122.62	−15 993.23	8 690.77	9 967.69
2001	−104.15	−49.08	−16 149.69	8 539.54	10 124.15
2003	−66.46	−26.62	−16 206.77	8 904.31	10 181.23
2005	−1.85	−0.62	−16 230.77	8 928.46	10 205.38
2007	−1.08	−0.31	−16 231.69	8 929.23	10 206.15

and so on). This reduction of charges follows the fluctuation of energy prices introduced in the programme annually.

The reduction in consumer expenses reached its highest level at ECU3.1 billion in 1983 (the price of a barrel of oil and the value of the dollar were at their maximum). It has stabilized since 1986 at around ECU1.1 billion per annum. It will regress quite rapidly beyond 1995 with the approaching end of equipment lifetime.

In the first column of Table 5.1, the reduction in expenses has been deflated and is expressed in 1992 money. In column 2, this value has been actualized to underline its economic importance. This calculation mode highlights past savings (which were operable in the economy up to now) and minimizes future savings. The cumulated value of the reduction in expenses (column 3) can be compared to the investments in energy management which have been deflated and actualized. The last two columns feature this return, for society taking all costs and savings into account and the consumer taking account of the subsidy.

We can infer the energy management return which describes the cumulative reduction in expenses once the equipment has been amortized :

- with regard to national economy:

    collective rent = reduction in expenses − investment

- with regard to the investor:

    investor return = reduction in expenses − (investment − subsidy)

From a macroeconomic point of view, the return reached a total of ECU8.9 billion for the 13 regions, that is, a rate of return of 196 per cent for all consumer sectors combined. From the consumers' point of view, the return reached ECU10 billion, giving an end of lifetime rate of return of 269 per cent (see Table 5.2).

We can then evaluate the profitability for the community of investing in these programmes. These important figures can be compared to the uncertain profitability of other heavy investments in the energy field: refineries, electric power stations, and so on. The latter can only be amortized over several decades, even when the hypotheses which led to their implementation prove to be correct. The substantial amounts achieved by energy savings, on the contrary, are rapidly recycled in the economy.

The uncertainties of the calculation
Several questions must be raised to validate this global calculation. Do the subsidies actually have an effect? Have the operations been functioning

Table 5.2 *Financial synthesis for all programmes*

	The 13 regions[a]		Extrapolation for France	
	1992 Value (in 1992 ECU million)	End of life value (in 1992 ECU million)	1992 Value (in 1992 ECU million)	End of life value (in 1992 ECU million)
Number of operations	2 982.62		~ 5 538	
Investments	3 117.85		~ 5 800	
Subsidies	580.62		~ 1 080	
Expenses annual decrease	513.23		~ 953	
Cumulated income of energy efficiency	7 040.92	8 929.23	~ 130 770	~ 16 597
Amortization without subsidies (%)	196	222		
Amortization with subsidies (%)	238	269		
Cumulated gain in hard currency	7 538.46	8 508.00	~ 14 015	~ 15 815

Note: [a] The 13 regions represent here 53.8 per cent.

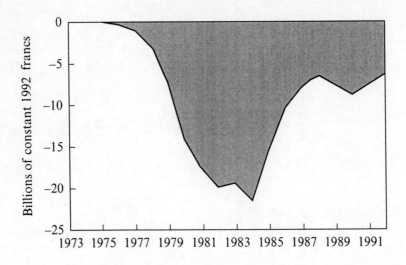

Source: ENERCOMPTA INESTENE, 1993.

Figure 5.1   Annual decrease in expenses induced by energy efficiency operations

correctly? Do they accurately represent the national programmes? Can the period considered be a model for the future?

The efficiency of the subsidies and their incentive character remain the most important puzzle in this kind of calculation. The problem arises when the benefit is attributed to the subsidy although the consumer would have invested anyway – the 'free-rider' effect. This difficulty, which occurred frequently when the subsidies were given routinely (after 1973), diminished markedly later due to the mode of functioning of the FSGT, which makes up most of this sample. Allocations from this fund were conditional upon a detailed calculation of the payback period; the operations with high profitability were excluded from the subsidy programme. We can also note that the aids to investment contributed to the modernization of the productive structure in the worst period of the crisis. In addition, they provided, for the service and commercial sector actors as well as for small enterprises, easier amortization after the drop in oil prices of 1986.

Moreover, the data collected here do not include the operations which did not receive any direct aid to investment, but were stimulated at least in part as a consequence of the preliminary studies which were paid for or the developments which were financed by the public authorities. Thus, the figures presented are

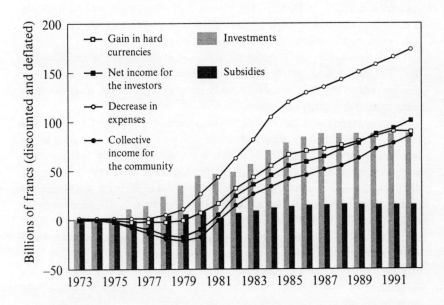

Source: ENERCOMPTA INESTENE, 1993.

Figure 5.2 Amortization of energy efficiency operations: all sectors (13 regions)

in this sense underestimated. Finally, the regulatory measures initiated during the period – insulation standards, boiler consumption and so on – also had an effect on costs and performance.

Since 1986, with the distancing of the state from energy management support, investments have dropped in this sector in spite of the fact that the market was expected to take over. The resulting weakening of consultancy firms and equipment suppliers has been associated with a reduction in the number of projects subsidized, to a greater extent than in neighbouring countries.

A second methodological issue is relevant: the characteristics of the operation are mainly described in the initial evaluation files. They are therefore *ex ante* data. In some cases, the files were updated on the basis of follow-ups (Poitou-Charentes, Aquitaine, Centre, Nord-Pas de Calais). The *ex post* evaluations carried out by the Agency were sufficient, however, to prove that the hypothetical efficiency of investments was reached on average for large operations. Enercompta's calculations are somewhat pessimistic and based on significant obsolescence at the outset, lifetime, and so on.

Only three significant *ex post* evaluations have been carried out in the 13 regions concerned. In Poitou-Charentes, a PhD thesis introduced a multiple criteria analysis model including, in particular, indirect economic effects, notably on local employment and on the environment.

The second study, of a sociological nature, was carried out in the Nord-Pas de Calais region. It established the level of satisfaction of the investors and its relation with investment payback periods. It shows a high level of satisfaction, often related to a variety of criteria.

The third study was carried out in Bretagne and established a correlation between the investment results and the forecast performances according to the level of involvement of the beneficiaries and their energy management competencies. It demonstrated that half the gains were related to the quality of decision and follow-through, the other half depending on the technical performance of the equipment used. Other smaller studies were undertaken in, for example, Alsace and Rhône-Alpes, with similar results. This underlines the importance of the role played by the regional teams in project negotiation and follow-through in training activities and so on.

These studies reveal that actual performance frequently matched expectations for large operations, notably industrial ones. By contrast, significant differences – up to 50 per cent – have been found in operations on small communal buildings, in agriculture, or when dealing with renewable energies. These disparities concerning small quantities of energy have only a negligible effect on the global results.

The representativeness of the sample and the national projection introduce few uncertainties. The regions represent close to half of the population, 53.8 per cent of energy consumption and 59.9 per cent of industrial production. Likewise, the number of projects, close to 20 000 in total, guarantees a representative character since, moreover, no particular type of investment was disregarded. Some projects resulted in insufficient profitability while others led to losses. This is the case for the 'return to coal' policies promoted by the Left government in the early 1980s, which lost all interest due to the drop in the price of heavy oil. Likewise, wood and heat recovery were clearly more profitable than investments in solar energy. Although some operations remain more profitable than others, our calculations include all operations of the period in the regions studied. It is therefore a representative series of public operations implemented over this long period.

In addition, no discrimination was introduced between the successive aid procedures. Aid to investment operations covers successive periods of high and low energy prices. Therefore the 1975–92 historical period can be considered to be representative of the ups and downs we will witness in the next decades.

Complementary approaches

The microeconomic cumulative gains presented above are not the only positive impacts to be taken in consideration. The policies can be evaluated by at least three other criteria: the gains in foreign exchange; the avoided pollutant emissions; and the macroeconomic effects on energy prices.

The calculation of the gains in foreign exchange due to a reduction of energy imports indicated that cumulative foreign exchange savings increased from 1.4 billion ECUs in 1981 to 7.7 billion in 1993, and an expectation that it would amount to 8.5 billion by 2005.

Regarding atmospheric pollution, the direct effects of the operations are substantial. The avoided emissions of atmospheric pollutants described hereafter were calculated in the following manner:

- the global masses of the emissions were counted, with the exception of carbon dioxide, of which only the mass of carbon was taken into account (this means dividing it by a factor 3.67);
- the figures presented hereafter result from the extrapolation of the figures for the 13 studied regions to the whole of France;
- the figures correspond to historical aggregations. They represent, for each year, the aggregation of the avoided emissions up to that point. This presentation gives an authentic image of the reduction of pollutants in the atmosphere prior to any absorption (by the ocean, for example);
- the dusts and sulphur oxide figures correspond to emissions prior to capture in de-pollution systems.

The results point to the following:

- the reduction of carbon dioxide emissions corresponded in 1992 to 3 per cent of French emissions. Moreover, these are only the reductions induced by the AFME's direct aid to investments;
- the slackening of avoided emission beginning in 1995 is a consequence of the decrease in energy management efforts;
- a low reduction of nitrogen oxide emissions, due to the small number of projects addressed to transportation.

These profitability rate and payback calculations depend on external factors such as the price of oil or other energies. After the oil counter-shock, the profitability of energy management operations, measured in a microeconomic manner in the accounts of enterprises, dropped. This analysis should be moderated in the light of results in all the European economies. The drop in prices is actually the result of the energy management policies implemented in the OECD countries. Thus, if these operations had not been carried out, in France and elsewhere, actors would have been confronted with much higher energy bills than they have today.

A macroeconomic comparison of the strategic constitution of oil and uranium stocks during the same period clearly demonstrates the advantage of energy savings. In some countries, such as France, this traditional strategy aimed to avoid the effects of an oil, gas or coal embargo. The same amounts invested in regulation stocks would have had a negative profitability rate and would even have had a detrimental effect on prices, first in terms of an increase, then of a decrease. By contrast, energy efficiency permitted the regulation of these prices while providing the same guarantees for security as before a crisis situation.

Finally, these programmes developed markets for new products whose extra costs were reduced. This factor has a positive effect on the equipment producers, but the extent has not been fully quantified.

Comparative Analysis of the Impact of the Different Procedures

Enercompta's data include, for each subsidy, the procedure which was used (400 francs/TOE, FSGT or FRME) and the date the operation began. We can thus attempt to interpret the impact of each of these procedures with regard to the institutional context of its implementation.

Let us recall that the three procedures can be distinguished in the following manner:

- *national aids proportional to the quantity of energy saved*: this system was applied until 1982, in the context of the centralization of procedures and allocated 400 francs per tonne of oil equivalent saved or substituted (around ECU60/TOE). It is therefore called the 400 francs/TOE programme;
- *aids proportional to the amount of the investments*: this cost-share principle was implemented massively with the Special Funds for Large Operations (FSGTs), invested by the French government in the early 1980s. These funds were allocated by the regional teams of the French Agency for Energy Management (AFME);
- *negotiated aids*: the amount of subsidy is directly negotiated with the partner according to the characteristics of each project. This system was applied for the Regional Funds for Energy Management (FRMEs) and the relevant funds of the French Agency for Energy Management (AFME) distributed since 1986.

We will undertake a comparative analysis according to three key points: the average size of the projects subsidised; the type of actor concerned; the profitability of the investments induced by the aids.

The average size of the projects

Table 5.3 gives data on subsidies and investments during three periods between 1975 and 1992. The first period, 1975–82, which essentially corresponds to the 400 francs/TOE period, is characterized by strong concentration of the subsidies: for fewer than 4000 projects evaluated, investments reached close to ECU2100 million, that is, almost as much as between 1982 and 1986 (FSGT and FRME procedures), where 25 000 operations were subsidized. The average investment in this first period reached ECU0.54 million, that is six times as much as in the second period. With an average subsidy rate of 13.5 per cent (compared to 25 per cent between 1982 and 1986), ECU282 million were distributed in the 1975–82 period while ECU574 million were distributed from 1982 to 1986.

Table 5.3 Subsidies and investments undertaken over three periods, 1975–92

Period	No. of operations	Subsidies (ECU million)	Investment (ECU million)	Average investment (ECU million)	Average subsidy (ECU million)
1975–82	3 873	282	2 097	0.54	0.072
1983–86	25 000	574	2 359	0.10	0.023
1987–92	3 435	84	592	0.17	0.024

The 400 francs/TOE automatic procedure clearly favoured the large projects. There are several reasons. First, the large, well-structured consumers were the first to grasp the stakes involved in investing in the rational use of energy. Second, they possessed the technical means to elaborate projects and implement them. Third, they certainly had easier access to information and to the administrative circles in charge of project evaluation. This preponderance of large projects was, moreover, quite consistent with the priorities of the period since the primary objective was to make massive savings, capable of reducing dependence on imported oil.

By comparison, the second period coincides with the implementation of AFME's regional delegations. This resulted in the strengthening of the door-to-door approach, technical assistance in the definition of projects, project monitoring for the least-structured economic actors, with the aim of disseminating technologies and know-how to encourage the rational use of energy in the economic system. The main objective then was to help each consumer to reduce the share of energy in his budget, whether it led to a gain in competitiveness by cutting production costs (in industry) or it reduced operating costs in favour of other priority budgetary items (in the service and commercial sector). The large projects were not excluded but were masked at the quantitative level behind numerous small projects pertaining to small enterprises, local authorities, and so on.

The following period (after 1986) coincides with a deep shift in the underlying philosophy. The aim was no longer extensively to support investments in the rational use of energy but, in a context of reduced energy prices and public energy efficiency budget cuts, to support the implementation of a limited number of innovative and demonstration operations. The allocation of subsidies was therefore more parsimonious (FFr546 million between 1987 and 1992), the amount was the object of negotiation with the beneficiaries, and led to a re-evaluation of the size of each project.

The type of actor concerned
The type of actor concerned in these different procedures varies according to the period. Industry was the main (and almost unique) beneficiary of the 400 francs/TOE programme, which supported modernization and adaptation to the new energy context by the large industrial groups. The SMEs had limited access to this procedure but benefited from aid to investments with the implementation of the FSGT and, to a smaller extent, the FRMEs. In a period in which large companies were increasingly taking their affairs into their own

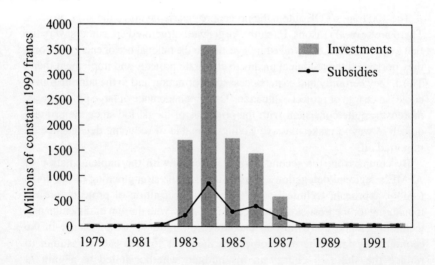

Source: ENERCOMPTA.

Figure 5.3   Annual investments and subsidies: the Special Fund for Large Operations (FSGT)

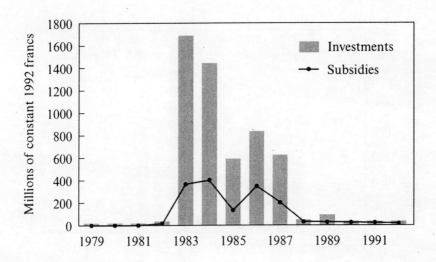

Source: ENERCOMPTA.

Figure 5.4 Annual investments and subsidies for the domestic and service sector

hands (numerous groups established energy specialists in their factories) and benefiting from soft loans through specialized financial institutions (SOFERGIES), the regional delegations developed consultancy and aid to decision-making activity that were better adapted to the SMEs and SMIs, either directly or step-by-step by setting up professional relays (audit and consultancy firms, specialized services in the local chambers of commerce, and so on). The role of the Agency was no longer limited to the evaluation of projects; it included activities upstream (to capture the attention of the consumers and inform them of technical possibilities) and downstream (to develop local capacity for the implementation of projects, to disseminate results in order to maximize the effects of the pilot operations).

This development of the Agency's activity has also furthered the development of service and commercial sector projects since 1982. These projects mainly concern the public or semi-public branches of this sector: education, health, social housing, municipal buildings, and so on.

The profitability of the investments induced by the subsidies
An examination of the raw figures (Table 5.4) shows that the average profitability of subsidized operations decreased over time and with the development of the

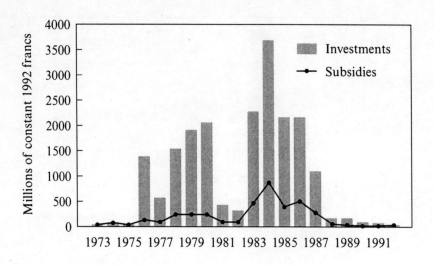

Source: ENERCOMPTA.

Figure 5.5   Annual investments and subsidies: all sectors

procedures. It might be presumed that the automatic procedures, not involving individualized promotion in the field, were more efficient than the decentralized ones. Three observations strongly qualify this statement:

- in general, the earlier that investments were made, the more profitable they were. The projects initiated later, in particular after the oil counter-shock of 1985–6, suffered a great deal from the conjectural decrease in profitability. Likewise, the oil savings of the first period were superseded later by energy substitutions, some of which were less profitable, such as the 'return to coal' programme which was compromised by the decrease in heavy fuel prices;

- thus, at the beginning of the first period, before the second oil crisis, the amortization was much higher than had been forecast in the initial projects. The operations were subsidized on the basis of oil prices before the increases. Investment profitability remained high until 1986. Industrial investments with small payback periods benefited most from this. In 1984 the annual induced return reached its highest level: ECU1.77 billion, thanks to a dollar at more than FFr10. The counter-shock took place in

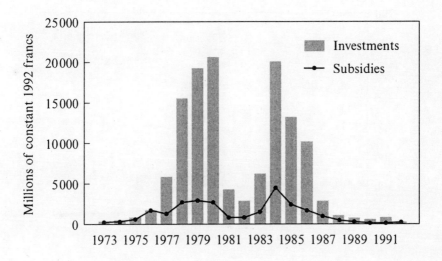

Source: ENERCOMPTA.

Figure 5.6   Anual investments and subsidies: industrial sector

1986. Savings remained quite profitable for fuel and electricity but subsidies targeted mainly thermal uses. The oil price drop from $35 to $18 per barrel in 1983 cut the return for energy management to one-third;

• the procedures used also had their effect: the bonuses allocated during the first period independently of investment profitability favoured, as we stated above, support to large industries in a period when investments were highly profitable. When the subsidies distributed are compared with the savings induced by the subsidized projects, profitability for the community appears to be high. However, it should be understood that, on the contrary, only a small part of these subsidies actually had a multiplying effect because this procedure probably contributed to projects which would have been implemented anyway: so-called 'free-riders'. The total lack of selectivity of the programme prevented it from limiting 'opportunist' demands. The profitability of public aid implemented during this period is probably far lower than it seems on first analysis.

The FSGT subsidies were also systematic but the mandatory payback period of the projects was more than five years. Thus, the most profitable projects were excluded from the programme at the outset (at the same time,

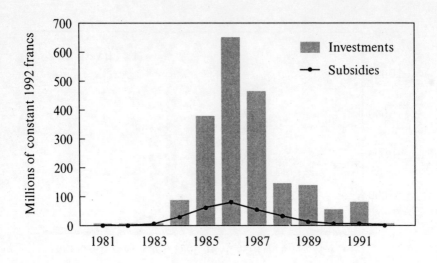

Source: ENERCOMPTA.

Figure 5.7   Annual investments and subsidies: regional energy management
*   funds (FRMEs)*

financial institutions were established to offer soft loans from the state to
enterprises). By definition, the FSGT thus limited its aid to the more 'risky'
projects, generally because they appeared innovative and cost-reducing
and would enable wider dissemination. The drop in profitability that can
be seen in the subsidized projects was therefore not necessarily a sign of
lower efficiency of the teams but, on the contrary, a product of better
selectivity of projects to benefit from non-reimbursable funds, the most
profitable projects being orientated towards more customized procedures,
less costly for the community.

   Finally, over the last period (1986–92), the decline in return is also linked
to the smaller financial capacities of the regional teams. In this context
of budgetary shortage, only the most innovative projects, for which aid
is indispensable, were subsidized. On average, the projects concerned were
much more risky and often non-profitable for the investor in a strict
economic sense. The subsidized projects, therefore, fall under a logic of
technological development and profitability should be analysed in terms
of long-term criteria such as the technical success of the projects and the
replication of technologies on a larger scale;

• the type of actor concerned: during the first period, only the large industrial operators had the technical means to benefit from the subsidies. Later, support reached the SMEs and the service and commercial sector, thanks to tools implemented in parallel with the subsidies: incentives to hire energy managers; the provision of training; and the establishment of technical centres, professional standards, and so on. The decreasing size of the projects also partially explains the decreasing profitability of the subsidies.

Table 5.4   Project returns for the three periods, 1975–92

Period of application	Subsidies (ECU million)	Investment (ECU million)	End of life amortization (with subsidy) (%)	Total cumulative average return (ECU million)
1975–82	282	2 097	373	14 503
1983–86	574	2 359	145	449
1987–92	84	592	98	−152

THE ACTIONS OF A REGIONAL TEAM

Different and Complementary Views of Intervention Aiming at Technological Dissemination

As can be observed, the French energy efficiency policy is rich in experience, which can be associated with the different views of public action.

Several views on technical dissemination co-exist in Europe. The following can be distinguished: a neo-liberal view which values the operation of the market; a belief that public subsidies can play the important role of catalyst; and a theory which advocates the organization of on-site actors. These three views will be presented briefly to set the stage for the discussion, before a detailed analysis of the components of local practice is introduced.

A neo-liberal view
Free market activity is advocated. In this view, the role of an administrative team intervening in a regional context primarily consists of informing the economic agents by disseminating information on efficient technologies. The investors can then make their own decisions according to market rules. If it is considered that the price system reflects costs, the allocation of public subsidies often appears useless and a sign of the excessive tendency of the state to interfere.

A public service theory through the allocation of public aids

The character of urgency of the oil shocks resulted in the establishment in most European countries of public teams allocating subsidies to encourage consumers to make energy savings. The objective of the subsidies was rapidly to trigger heavy investment. The state thus sought to set up simple administrative decision procedures. The allocation of public aid through 'ticket-office' procedures was identified as the condition for energy efficiency dissemination. The effectiveness of this method was questioned when oil prices decreased and states, confronted with the economic crisis, reduced their financial efforts.

A view based on the organization of on-site actors

This underlines the fragmentation of the demand-side compared to the supply-side actors. The organization of branches requires parallel organization of the actors. As a consequence, the aim is to help executives to make decisions and to structure professions, and not to subsidize limited projects. Therefore, it is necessary to stress the multiplicity of instruments to deal with various situations. Public intervention is, thus, justified as a transitory adjustment method which not only corrects market 'imperfections' but is also a dynamic structuring process.

The 400 francs/TOE procedure   This was a centralized 'ticket office' system with no true technical added value from the teams in charge of project evaluation. It is clearly linked to the second category. From its results, four lessons may be learned:

1. The extreme simplicity of the evaluation procedure brought about a large number of investments. The large industrial groups quickly perceived the advantages they could draw from this programme. Because there was no minimum payback period, many existing projects were brought out of the closet and submitted for subsidies. Moreover, the procedure actually ended up anticipating investments, which is a mediocre way of spending public funds. However, the circumstances were favourable: large industrial groups began to invest in massive heavy oil savings during the months before the second oil crisis, thus lessening its consequences. This procedure had the advantage of being transparent and equitable as a rule, because all investors had access to public funds under the same conditions.
2. However, the programme had little effect on the dissemination of innovation. Its mechanical character favoured the most commonplace solutions: substituting boilers; installing exchangers; recovering the calorific power contained in smoke or insulating the ovens, and so on.
3. The space-heat installers used this bonus as a commercial advantage regardless of the energy quality of the equipment they were selling (quite often boilers). What we can gather here is that an intermediary cannot play

its true role of recommendation if it has a financial interest in any work induced. Moreover, they needed to be supervised; without this, the bonuses given to individuals had little effect.

4. The lack of involvement of the regional actors led to an insufficient horizontal dissemination of technologies and know-how (a very low multiplying effect from sector to sector).

The FSGT programme This programme corresponds to a combination of two theories: a massive dissemination of public subsidies backed by an effort of organization of on-site partners, ensuring the emergence of less-conventional projects involving a larger number of small operators and ensuring better dissemination of information on successful experiences. This procedure had the following effects:

1. It improved the technical quality of the evaluation of the projects (to avoid overestimation of the forecast savings by the consultancy firms preparing the dossiers).
2. There was improved allocation of public subsidies (to avoid financing operations with very small payback periods, to deduct additional costs which were not eligible for subsidies from the eligible investments, and so on).
3. The massive character of the subsidies rapidly created a market for new products (for example, exchangers, mechanical vapour recompression, gas condensation boilers).
4. However, the stress put on rapidity of evaluation of the projects favoured simple techniques or sufficiently mature ones to be disseminated on the market, to the detriment of operations whose implementation would take longer. Thus, there were very few projects taking advantage of renewable energies.

The FRMEs These are linked to the last category above, and favour dialogue and negotiation, local action, the establishment of networks of operators, intermediaries and partners of the public Agency. We can make the following appraisal of this programme:

1. The FRMEs had a much larger multiplying effect than the massive aids to investment on the development of sectors. Thus, a large number of small enterprises were involved.
2. They contributed more effectively to the development of quite innovative operations, independently of their short-term profitability. The effort was concentrated on promising activities not yet taken up by the market because of cost constraints, or on the dissemination of know-how. The subsidized operations had, in this framework, a strong character of demonstration.

Where projects succeeded, the complementary procedures of aid to investment, such as communication, training and so on, increased the multiplying effect (induced effect).

3. However, in cases where the qualifying criteria for aid were less transparent than the preceding ones, benefits were only available to a small circle of partners.

The Elements of Regional Practice

We have observed how the same instrument (aid to investment) may be used in three different institutional contexts, involving to a greater or lesser degree the regional intermediaries. We will now discuss and differentiate the main components of local practice and then detail more precisely the underlying logic of the concepts observed. Finally, we will evaluate the economic multiplying effect of a regional team in charge of disseminating energy efficiency technologies.

The orientations

The level of planning of objectives with political partners   France is a special case due to the weakness of regional energy planning, compared with federally structured countries, or countries where local authorities are strong to the extent that central authorities do not define the global objectives in terms of energy or the environment (for instance, a level of emission which should be reached in 10 or 20 years). This absence of perspective leads to an incapacity to frame regionally defined action programmes. This results, at the outset, in an actual political weakness each time the representatives or the administrative executives request coherent financial means from the regional authority for its action programme, with regard to clearly defined priorities.

A regional policy will therefore consist of involving the regional actors in energy efficiency action planning based on medium-term quantitative objectives, for instance, a commitment to reduce greenhouse gas emissions according to the objectives accepted by the countries which ratified the Climate Convention after the Rio Conference.

But action should not be deferred until the completion of objective planning and the formulation of a regional energy perspective. The quality of these efforts depends precisely on the experience of those on the ground who are making them.

The comparison of the energy alternatives   The main function of a regional team is to allow energy consumers to compare competitive energy alternatives by searching for the most efficient technologies adapted to particular uses. Past experience has shown that this objective is easy to achieve each time the competition between energies is strong, for thermal uses for example, and when some means of comparison are available to the consumers (an internal competency for the larger organizations). This was the case in industry, large local authorities, hospitals, the social housing bodies, and so on. This rational decision-making capability was much weaker for small industrial firms, the service and commercial sector and households.

The specific uses to which electricity and oil are put present greater difficulties. No competition mechanisms encourage energy savings. Therefore, the electricity utilities as well as automobile manufacturers openly push consumption. This abuse, which is based on their dominant market situation, must be corrected by implementing demand-side management programmes for electricity use and also comparison between transportation modes, notably in urban areas.

The actors

The capacity to contract with the territorial authorities   A capacity to contract is absolutely indispensable. It gives regional teams greater flexibility regarding the administrative structures. This contracting concerns two types of activities: planning (objective contracts with long, medium or short-term programmes) and project design (including the designation of institutional partners as intermediaries).

The intermediary policy   A small local energy-efficiency dissemination team cannot limit its activities to its own staff. Intermediaries must be set up to multiply the effect of its action. There should be more intermediaries as targeted energy consumers become more dispersed.

This policy presupposes that project analysis and aids to decision-making methods have been standardized. Two types may appear: the establishment of direct intermediaries and the use of existing ones. The second solution is preferable for two reasons: first, by associating with existing intermediaries the permanent structure costs are reduced; second, collaboration with a well-established structure in the targeted sector facilitates the association of energy conservation with other criteria, such as recommendations to the consumer on housing issues, and the dissemination of innovative technologies by technical centres of industrial branches.

This is a crucial point of local policy. Actor networks are too rarely assessed: an actor database would be a useful tool to follow the activities of local teams.

There may be both public institutional and private professional or associative intermediaries; for example:

- consumer associations, to increase the awareness of tenants and landlords to energy savings;
- local authorities, so that energy is taken into consideration during real-estate transactions (the establishment of a thermal audit before the purchase) and when issuing the building permits;
- domestic appliance equipment suppliers, to disseminate the most efficient equipment;
- professional technical centres for technical training in industry.

Communication and leadership policies

Far too frequently, communication policies consist in searching for a high profile by enhancing the public image. This indispensable approach at the national level has a low cost:efficiency ratio at the local level. Communication policies should primarily enhance actor networks and help energy consumers find the appropriate intermediaries. They should also participate in the spread of knowledge concerning subsidies.

The tools

Consistency, transparency and simplicity in decision-making procedures
Significant benefits are yielded by standardization of methods. Thus, the thermal audit method invented in 1980 by ANAH constituted, in France, a tool recognized by all to validate energy savings investment projects in existing buildings. This is all the more important where targeted energy consumers have weak internal capacities to identify opportunities and to act on them.

The role of a local team is less to do things than to get things done; it cannot do everything itself. It is here that the link with the national structure (Agency, research service) is vital. The analytical gaps to be filled include: aid to local planning (zoning regulations, urban development schemes); aid to decision-making in transportation infrastructure planning; demand-side management implementation in electricity; and the use of renewable energies.

Expertise and project implementation services   This know-how is more specific than the dissemination of consultancy methods. The quality of the expertise is the result of experience acquired through addressing multiple realities, whether technical, economic, institutional or social. Expertise can only be effective where there is some benchmark or basis of comparison, that is, project and policy evaluation. For example, it is difficult for the leaders of a municipality to decide about the construction of a domestic waste treatment facility with energy recovery when they have no previous experience.

One justification for using expertise is to discern the causes of failure. Too often, public authorities, hooked on justifying implemented policies, ignore them.

The proliferation of poor practice in the field of renewable energies in the absence of this necessary vigilance has been quite detrimental to some activities: thermal solar, waste gasification, and so on.

The integration of activities from upstream to downstream, bringing demonstration projects from research to dissemination The dissemination of innovative techniques inevitably entails the articulation of regional experience, sometimes profession by profession. The activity of a local team consists in presenting the results of demonstration operations to potential partners.

Increasingly, demonstration operations are in part funded by European Union programmes (THERMIE, DG XVII). They ensure the availability of greater expertise and permit a broader dissemination of the results than was possible heretofore. The success of this dissemination depends in part on the quality of the *ex post* evaluations made.

One-off efforts cannot ensure the dissemination of innovative technologies. They require a network of competent actors throughout the entire sector. A local team will thus seek to identify the weak links and, as a priority, contribute to their reinforcement. Hence, while fuel wood in certain circumstances is quite competitive, its use is declining. This is the result in part of defective articulation of the links which range from forest resources to the installation of boilers (no guarantee of supply, the absence of specialized commercial and bank services, a lack of insurance for risk sharing).

Financing measures

The means of dissemination and administrative procedures regulating access to financing These have changed radically over recent years:

- *Uniform administrative procedures* After the oil shocks, uniform administrative procedures were set up to support investment. In France, the conditions for access to these funds were directly decided by the ministries. The local teams charged with their implementation could not adapt them (for example, in relation to subsidy rates or qualifying conditions). This type of financing presented two strengths and two weaknesses. The strengths are the transparency of the procedure and the democratic access to it. The weaknesses are the risk of inadequacies in regard to the specific realities on the ground and poor technical quality resulting from bureaucratic evaluation which often sacrifices innovation to the rigidity of the administrative procedure.
- *Procedures decided on a local level* Financial disinvestment by the state in the mid-1980s was accompanied by the discontinuation of the above-mentioned procedures and their replacement by case-by-case

decision modes with quite flexible evaluation criteria. These have the inverse qualities and weaknesses of the above. Improved adaptability to the actual conditions of a project is an advantage as long as the evaluations justify public involvement. There is a high risk that the allocation of subsidies may become arbitrary. In some situations, the beneficiaries of public subsidies can become a restricted circle of privileged interlocutors who are aware of the implicit criteria applied in decision-making.

- *Financing modalities according to the nature of the resources (subsidies on the public budget, parafiscal taxes)*   The nature of the financial resources has an influence on project design. Parafiscal taxes ensure stable financing and thus permit pluriannual planning. Budgetary resources from the state imply relatively uniform procedures. Credits from the Council of the European Communities mainly enhance innovation. Contracting with the territorial authorities tends towards a better 'fit' to the realities on the ground. It is clear that the diversification of financing modalities is essential to the elaboration of a complete policy. However, a local team tends to limit itself spontaneously to the financial boundaries of its own structure.
- *The building of financial partnerships with banks and third-party financal bodies*   Assistance in making financial arrangements becomes a crucial skill as state financing and the availability of subsidies declines. It is necessary now to consider a regional team as a focus of intellectual resource and expertise capable of designing projects, even if their financing is undertaken totally by private operators.

The evaluation

The evaluation of the implemented policies   Evaluation of the policies plays a double role. The first is to validate technical performance and thereby reassure the partners (public authorities, bankers, investors, and so on). The second consists in providing financial and economic justification. Public financial resources are scarce; the investment criteria must be clearly defined.

The evaluation must inevitably be based on multiple criteria. Its object is to research the dysfunctionalities at least as much as the causes of success, for there are valuable lessons to be learnt from experience. Standardization will help ensure that evaluations can be compared.

A focus on outputs rather than inputs   The legitimacy of the actions of a local team lies in the allocation of public funds. Its efficiency must be judged in terms of the actual results regarding energy and environmental performance.

The Dominant Logic

From this presentation we can infer the following types of logic:

- *an administrative logic* within which the local level functions primarily as an administrator of public fund allocations decided at a national level. The efficiency of this mode is all the stronger where the structure is national, perennial and possesses codified procedures and substantial financial means. The prototype of this functioning mode was the AFME during the FSGT period;
- *an 'as the world turns' logic* which consists of responding to demand, without precise planning of actions and without a public procedure that organizes the financing regulations. This logic leaves a lot of initiative to local teams but becomes less tenable as energy concern becomes of secondary importance. This mode has often characterized the regional energy agencies;
- *a logic of management by objectives* where the objective, procedures and establishment of intermediaries are negotiated globally with the partners with the aim of structuring local demand. The institutional and financial legitimacies are played down in favour of the will to develop activities.

The Multiplying Effect of a Regional Team

Let us assume, as a case study, a region of around 2 million inhabitants setting up a team of 15 to 20 people to guide its energy conservation policy. We will identify its cost, its activity and the multiplying effect that can be expected from the experience acquired. At this stage, the source of legitimacy of this team is of no importance (it could be a regional energy agency established by a regional assembly, a team established in the region by a ministry or a state agency).

The cost of a 15-person team (salaries, premises, operating costs) runs to about ECU1 million (1994) per year. This expense will be, one way or the other, a charge on a public authority. What are the positive impacts of this team's action which can be presented to balance these expenses? From the simplest to the most complicated, they are: the reduction of the authority's own energy expenses; the expenses of the regional economic actors; the enhancement of local resources; the beneficial effects on employment; and the environmental benefits.

It has proved quite difficult to quantify the actions of a regional team. The following figures must be put into perspective. They are based on an 'average' of the situations observed in the various regions during the evaluations. This quantification is easy to make for the 'ticket office' type of administrative evaluation for aids to investment. Experience shows that a team of 20 people can monitor yearly 200 operations (from evaluation to aid to investment). The

Table 5.5 Economic efficiency of a local team (ECU thousand)

	Public contribution (operations and subsidies)	Induced investments	Public intervention investments	Energy impact 10^3 toe	Induced decrease in expenses: investment lifetime	Public intervention: cumulative decrease in expenses
Annual running costs of the team	1 500					
Aids to investment, industry	1 200	9 000	0.13	10 000	15 000	0.08
residential, commercial, agricultural and renewables	1 200	4 850	0.25	1 120	7 300	0.16
Branch organization	380	5 000	0.08	3 133	7 400	0.05
Total	4280	18 850	0.23	14 253	29 700	0.14

The overall collective balance is thus (in ECU thousands):

Public expense	4 280
Private expense (investment + subsidy)	16 450
Total expense	20 730
Decrease in expenses (actualized to 8%)	29 700
Net actualized value	8 970

Gains in CO_2 (10^3 tonnes)	1 900
Gains in SO_2 (10^3 tonnes)	36
Gains in NO_x (10^3 tonnes)	3

economic impact varies according to the consuming economic sector. The amount of investment in industry is around ECU0.23 million, whereas in the domestic sector it reaches ECU15 000. The investment multiplier for subsidies for conservation falls in the range 5–10 (with the exception of demonstration operations, which require more extensive aid). Therefore, we can estimate the induced activity (investment by the operators) at around ECU20 to 25 million per year with a subsidy volume of ECU2.5–5 million. It should be noted that the subsidies to be allocated are of the same order of magnitude as the VAT collected by the state on these operations.

Another return to the national economy is in terms of the reduction of hard currency expenses. If we estimate the value of a TOE in oil at 85 ECU, a savings of 1 TOE with a 15-year lifetime saves ECU920.

A local team does not only find its justification through direct aid to investment. As we have seen, its action mainly consists of structuring activities and stimulating project emergence. More and more, the tendency is for investment financing to pass through bank products, such as third-party financing, without any public subsidy.

The judgement which should be made on a regional energy-efficiency promotion team does not, however, change; but clearly a radical transformation needs to be made in administrative mentalities. The justification of the action of a public team should not be linked solely to its capacity to spend public money but to its benefit to society as a whole. Hence, the importance of evaluating the results rather than the inputs.

A project designer with a yearly organization budget of ECU75 000 can contribute to the reinforcement of some technical activity, whether by technical studies, participant training, preparation of the financial set-up, or evaluations of the outcomes or obstacles encountered. We can estimate an average rate of concrete operations at 20. This figure can vary considerably as between industry, the residential sector, renewable energies, electricity savings, and so on. This form of intervention could be particularly effective for activities where split investments are the rule.

The above can be summarized as follows: A 15-person team, comprising five people in charge of administration, five managers for projects whose investment schemes have previously been set up and five branch organizers, will yield the cost and return characteristics shown in Table 5.5.

NOTES

1. TOE = tonne of oil equivalent, MTOE = millions of tonnes of oil equivalent.
2. Methodological note : For industry, the 13 regions studied by Enercompta represented, in 1982, an industrial energy consumption of 27 183 604 kTOE, that is, 54.2 per cent of the entire country (50 132 074 kTOE). In 1990, the share of the 13 regions was close to 60 per cent. In

terms of active population, these 13 regions represent 54 per cent of the active population employed in French industry. The results from Enercompta concerning the industrial sector are divided by 0.60 to give the figures for the whole of France. This distribution is detailed, for example, for agricultural and food industries (58.5 per cent of the total for France) and for paper and cardboard industries (70.5 per cent of the total), and so on. For the domestic and service sector, the 13 regions represented 51 per cent of the global consumption of this sector for France in 1990. This proportion is almost equal for the population, that is, 29.127 million inhabitants (51.7 per cent). For agriculture, the share is 57.2 per cent and for transportation 51.4 per cent. It should be noted that these projections were made in final energies calculated according to the French equivalency system. The respective shares of energies hardly vary from one region to another over the period; the results thus remain equivalent to those of the international system.

3. For each of the operations processed by Enercompta, the energy prices were introduced in the calculation from the evaluation period up to 1992, according to price fluctuations by consumer sector and by energy quality. Beyond 2010, the Energy Observatory's 'low scenario' hypotheses have been adopted.

6. Summary and conclusions

Frank J. Convery

THE POLICY INSTRUMENTS ANALYSED

The following policy instruments were analysed:

- *grants/subsidies* to encourage investment in conservation of energy in domestic housing and direct investment in public buildings (ESRI, Dublin);
- *information*, to inform householders in Germany concerning their conservation options and their implications (Fraunhofer Institut, Karlsruhe);
- *regulation*, applied as a means of encouraging combined heat and power in the Netherlands and other EU countries (Department of Science, Technology and Society, University of Utrecht, and SEO, University of Amsterdam);
- *demand-side management* by utilities as a means of achieving conservation in lighting (Association for the Conservation of Energy, London);
- *institutional development*, as a means of engendering 'bottom up' conservation initiatives (ICE and INESTENE, Paris).

METHODOLOGY

Ex post analysis of the application of each instrument was undertaken. The primary focus was on in-depth analysis of the experience in one member state which had utilized the instrument in question and for which some data were available; but the experiences in other member states and elsewhere in the world were also drawn upon.

Main Assumptions

- Where feasible, the main *commercial or private benefit* evaluated was the value of the energy saved. Where possible, the free-rider benefits – the

143

benefits which would have been yielded with or without the policy instrument in question – are identified;
- the benefits (and costs) were valued at current prices paid by purchasers, expressed in 1994 ECUs, except where shadow pricing was clearly called for and was feasible;
- the costs were estimated as the total public and private outlays (capital and current) needed to achieve the conservation;
- where relevant, future costs and returns were capitalized at an interest rate of 8 per cent, but other rates were also used.

Much of the analysis in this book derives not from original work but from existing analyses. The assumptions underlying these studies vary. We have made every effort to achieve as much consistency as possible across studies; but inevitably, the reader should allow a considerable margin of error in comparing across countries and across time.

Valuing External Benefits of Energy Conservation

The estimated *public or external benefits* of conservation were the projected reduction in annual emissions of carbon dioxide (CO_2), sulphur dioxide (SO_2), nitrogen oxides (NO_x) and (where available) volatile organic compounds (VOC) and carbon monoxide (CO), and employment (person years).

Some provisional (and partial) estimates of external costs associated with electric power generation have been estimated per kWh of electricity produced (see Table 6.1).

Table 6.1   Damage estimates associated with different fuel cycles (mECUs per kWh)

Damage category	Coal (Germany)	Gas power station (UK)
Health		
Public	13.00	0.5
Occupational	2.0	0.1
Accidents (agriculture)	0.04	Not quantified
Materials damage	0.10	0.1
Total	15.14	0.7

Source: CEC (1994).

A number of other benefits – reduction in timber losses, reduction in damage to terrestrial and marine ecosystems, landscape effects – have not yet been evaluated. The evaluation of greenhouse gas effects in Table 6.2 was taken from a number of existing studies.

Table 6.2 Valuation of external benefits of reducing greenhouse gases in power generation (mECUs per kWh)

Source[a]	Fuel (mECU/kWh)	
	Coal	Gas
Cline (1992)	15	6
Fankhauser (1993)	10	4
Tol (1995)	18	8
Hohmeyer and Gartner (1992)	5000	2100

Note: [a] Sources listed are detailed in the References to Chapter 1.

Source: CEPN *et al.* (1994, p. 161).

The methodology has the great benefit of providing insights into real, as opposed to hypothetical, experience. The weakness is that policy is always initiated and implemented during a period when other factors which influence performance also change: energy prices, the implementation of other policy instruments which affect performance, expectations about the future, the compctence of the implementation process, rising or falling disposable income, are examples of such factors. But part of the art of the policy process is to make judgements concerning such matters, to ensure that policy is carried out in the context of a mix of exogenous and endogenous events which will yield a net gain.

SUBSIDY AND DIRECT INVESTMENT

Policies implemented in Ireland, the UK, the Netherlands, Germany and Denmark were analysed. The results are summarized below (Table 6.3):

Ireland: Subsidies for Households and Investment in Government Buildings

The following conclusions can be drawn from the Irish experience with subsidies and direct investment:

• they give a very good rate of return on investment, but the total volume is very small. The attic insulation and the low-income household schemes were taken up by 29 000 and 1200 households respectively, out of a total number of approximately 1 million;

- by focusing on specific conservation opportunities, it was possible to avoid the 'diversion' of public funds to other types of home improvement;
- the government investment in hospitals and office buildings was undertaken as pilot projects. But the implications – good rates of return – do not seem to have been acted upon; institutional failure to create the appropriate incentive structures seem to be to blame;
- the attic insulation subsidy was available to all householders; it is likely that it was made use of 'disproportionately' by the higher income groups;
- the benefit estimates are based on the projections of experts, not on actual performance. In particular, we do not know to what extent householders took the benefits of improved insulation in the form of more heat rather than reduced energy consumption.

Table 6.3   Results from a number of subsidy and direct investment programmes in energy conservation, Ireland, (1994 ECU million)

Category	Total costs	Ann. benefits	Payback (yrs)	Employment (Person/yrs)	CO_2 reduction (000 tonnes)
Attic insulation subsidy grant scheme (1980–82)	9497	2677	3.50	200	50
Insulation of low income households (1993–94)					
(Energy Action)	293	118	2.50	+	0.344
Government investment					
Office buildings	71	20	3.48	+	0.360
Hospitals	875	705	1.80	Neg.	6.800

Notes:
1. No allowance has been made for 'free-riders'.
2. Some estimates were also made of other environmental emissions.
3. The attic insulation scheme provided maximum grant of ECU120 per household; total grants paid out amounted to ECU3 million.
4. The insulation of low-income households under 'Energy Action' was designed mainly as a training scheme for the long-term unemployed, and dealt with about 1200 households. It is assumed that the opportunity cost of labour is zero.
5. The + in the 'Employment' column signifies an unquantified gain.

UK: Subsidies for Households

The results are summarized below (Table 6.4):

Home Energy Efficiency Scheme (HEES)
The scheme provides grants for low-income housing for basic insulation (draught insulation, loft insulation and energy advice) up to a maximum of ECU400 per household. Over 600 000 out of a total eligible population of 6.4 million households have taken up the grant. The scheme is administered by a

private non-profit company, the Energy Action Grant Agency. Over 1800 full-time equivalent staff are involved in installation and so on, and the work is carried out by locally based charities; Heatwise in Glasgow is one of these, and has worked in over 70 000 households in the city.

Table 6.4   Performance of the Home Energy Efficiency Scheme, UK

Actual average cost per household (ECU)	180
Potential annual savings (ECU)	50
Potential payback period (years)	3.5
Actual savings (ECU)	11
Actual payback period (years)	16

Note: The potential payback period was based on the premise that dwellings were heated to 'full comfort conditions' before and after. In practice, it seems that houses were underheated before insulation, and that most householders have taken most of the benefits of insulation in the form of increased heat.

The Green House programme
The objective of the programme was to establish a network of energy-efficient demonstration projects to improve the energy efficiency of local authority housing. Because it was a demonstration project, the results (see Tables 6.5 and 6.6) were carefully monitored.

Table 6.5   Performance of the Green House programme, UK

No. of projects	180
Energy savings (% reduction)	42
CO_2 Emissions reduction (%)	56
Aggregate payback period (years)	7.7

Table 6.6   Performance of sample energy conservation projects

	York	Enfield	Hove
Total costs (ECU000)	20	96	321
Annual benefits (ECU000)	2	21	23
Payback period (years)	8	4.6	13.9
CO_2 reduction (tonnes)	16	119	88

Note: In York, four houses were treated, including general insulation, window replacement and heating system installation (including one less than successful heating pump). In Enfield, incandescent lighting was replaced by CFLs in communal areas. In addition to energy savings, better lighting improved feelings of security and reduced vandalism. The Hove project involved installing new heating systems, double glazing, insulation, and ventilation with heat recovery. The latter was innovative and posed problems of operation, and this reduced performance.

The key lessons of the Green House projects are that the 'tried and tested' technologies – as in Enfield – provided much better returns than the innovative systems – as in Hove; much of the benefit was in the form of improved performance rather than reduced energy consumption; effective tenant consultation and advice proved of vital importance: providing leaflets was not sufficient.

The Netherlands: Subsidies for Energy Conservation in Housing

The National Insulation Programme was initiated in 1979 to cover double glazing and insulation of cavity walls, floors and roofs, with a maximum subsidy of ECU850 per dwelling. From 1987, it became part of a house improvement scheme. In 1982, it became clear that the scheme was not attractive to owners and occupiers of rented accommodation; Dutch landlords are allowed to increase rents following improvements in dwellings, but must first get the permission of the tenant(s) to make the improvement. This combined to inhibit take-up from this component of the residential sector. As a result, grants to the rented sector were increased, so that the rents would need to increase by less as a result of investments by landlords. Grants to owner-occupiers were abolished.

There are at present grants available (ECU3–5 per kW of new capacity) for the replacement of existing boilers by high-efficiency and low-emission central heating boilers, and a fixed grant for insulation and double glazing.

There were no data available on performance.

Germany: Grants and Tax Rebates for Energy Conservation

This programme ran from mid-1978 to mid-1983, and provided a grant or a tax allowance. The grant covered 25 per cent of the investment cost, for investments in the range ECU3000–9000 per dwelling. The tax allowance amounted to 10 per cent of the investment cost for ten years. Allowable expenditure included insulation and improvements in heating systems in houses built before 1978 and innovative heating systems for all houses. Most of the budget was used for improved insulation, 77 per cent on double glazing.

Table 6.7   Performance of German subsidy programme for energy conservation in households

Participation	(no. of households)	1.51 million
Total costs	(ECUbillion)	18–19
Annual savings	(ECUbillion)	0.8
Payback period	(years)	>20
CO_2 reduction	(million tonnes)	6

Box 6.1

Lessons for policy-makers in the use of subsidy and direct investment to achieve energy conservation

1. *This instrument can yield substantial net benefits if certain conditions are met.*

2 *The investment subsidy must be focused narrowly on the most cost-effective opportunities.*
   In Germany, performance was poor because the subsidy for householders subvented window replacement and the installation of double glazing, where the energy payoff per ECU invested was much less than was yielded in Ireland and the UK, where only draught-proofing and ceiling insulation was grant-aided.

3. *The net energy conservation gain from household conservation programmes is modest, but comfort gains are substantial.*
   Households are not heated to full comfort conditions before insulation, therefore, much of the benefit is taken in the form of increased comfort.

4. *A mechanism is needed for learning and applying the lessons of pilot schemes.*
   In Ireland, pilot schemes showed large net gains to conservation investment in hospitals and some government buildings, but these lessons were not internalized and acted upon.

5. *There are considerable economies of scale.*
   In the UK, the Home Energy Efficiency Scheme was taken up by 600 000 households; the overhead cost per household was minimal.

Note: This information is based on the detailed analysis in Chapter 1.

The payback judged in terms of energy savings is extremely poor (see Table 6.7). This may be accounted for by the fact that most of the money went on double glazing, which is not a very cost-effective use of conservation funds, and some funding was used for window replacement. In addition, many householders are likely to have taken their benefit in the form of improved heat rather than reduced energy consumption.

INFORMATION AND MOTIVATION: THE GERMAN EXPERIENCE

Since 1978, householders in Germany have had available a free consultancy service on energy conservation options. Information is provided in three fashions: information is provided through drop-in centres and mobile buses, and since 1992 site visits by energy experts are grant-aided to 95 per cent of total costs up to a maximum of ECU475. Five per cent of households have used the advice centres at least once, but very few have availed themselves of the site visit, perhaps because the grant level is regarded as too low for a comprehensive analysis.

In the State of Hessen, three means of providing information – written advice, personal audits, and the use of chimney sweeps (every chimney in Germany has to be swept once a year) – were analysed. The details re the unit costs of the alternatives are summarized in Table 6.8.

Table 6.8   Costs and cost effectiveness of alternative information transmission systems, Hessen, Germany

	No. of responses	Total cost (ECU)	Cost per case (ECU)	Savings (kWh/ECU)
Written advice	83	12 500	75	320
Personal audits	227	475 000	560	38
Chimney sweeps	445	90 000	75	250

Note: The savings are per ECU spent on the consultation.

Table 6.9   Energy conservation expenditure and projected energy savings, by information medium per participating household, Hessen, Germany

	Avg. investment (ECU)	Avg. energy savings (kWh)	Energy saving (kWh/ECU)
Written advice	6000	7000	1.17
Personal audit	8000	8000	1.00
Chimney sweeps	6000	4500	0.75

The respondents were asked what investments they had made in the light of the recommendations; the energy-saving potential was then estimated. On the basis of these analyses, projections were made of the costs and energy savings (see Table 6.9). Clearly, the written advice yields the largest payoff in energy saved per ECU invested, and it is also the cheapest means of information transmission. There seems to be no value added by the site visit. The advice of the chimney sweeps is skewed in favour of new boilers and against insulation (see Table 6.10).

Table 6.10   Investments undertaken as a percentage of recommendations made

	New boilers	Central heating control	Insulated windows	Cellar ceiling insulation
Written analysis	66	61	79	20
Personal audit	74	75	67	21
Chimney sweep	76	62	45	13

The conclusions resulting from the analysis of information as a policy instrument are as follows:

• some media are much more cost-effective than others; in the case of Hessen, written analysis is much cheaper than the alternatives and seems to yield about the same levels of energy conservation;
• bias in the nature of the advice given can skew the advice. In the German case, chimney sweeps seemed to advise new boilers more than the typically more cost-effective ceiling and window insulation.

Box 6.2
Lessons for Policy-makers on the use of information and education to achieve energy conservation

1. *Written advice, based on a response to a completed questionnaire, is the most cost effective means of transmitting information about energy conservation opportunities to households.*
   The Hessen study shows that the take-up of advice is similar for written advice (completed at an advice centre), personal audits and chimney sweeps. However, the written reply is much less expensive than the personal audit and provides less-biased advice than the sweep.

2. *Conservation advice from chimney sweeps may be biased in favour of boiler replacement and central heating control.*
   The Hessen study showed that these relatively expensive options tend to be favoured over less expensive choices such as cellar ceiling insulation.

Note: This information is based on the detailed analysis in Chapter 2.

REGULATION: THE CASE OF COMBINED HEAT AND POWER (CHP)

Compared to the separate generation of heat and power, CHP saves 30 per cent compared with a conventional power plant, and 15 per cent when it replaces natural gas-fired combined cycles. But the share of CHP in most EU countries is static or falling; the Netherlands and Denmark are the exceptions.

Heat is used to generate steam or hot water. Because heat cannot be transported as easily as electricity, for private producers demand for heat is the key to determining output of both electricity and heat. When more electricity is produced than is needed for own consumption, this can either be sold to the grid or to another user(s) by transporting it via the grid (wheeling). When the CHP unit is not in production, electricity must be purchased from the grid.

Table 6.11   Industrial installed combined heat and power capacity by country, 1989

Country	Installed capacity (MWe)
Germany	8450
Italy	4630
France	1980
Netherlands	1820
UK	1793
Spain	962
Portugal	388
Belgium	340
Denmark	140
Ireland	58
Greece	40

The industrial installed capacity in 1989 is shown in Table 6.11. However, the share of CHP-produced electricity in the total has been falling (see Table 6.12).

Table 6.12   Combined heat and power share of EU electricity production, 1974 and 1990

Year	Total electricity production (TWh)	CHP-related production (TWh)	CHP as % of total
1974	1150	103	9
1990	1800	103	6

There has been growth only in Denmark and the Netherlands; Germany, France and Belgium all show a decline. Denmark and the Netherlands (Table 6.13) are the countries which have committed most policy effort to encouraging CHP, with the result that they are the only countries showing growth in this regard.

Table 6.13　Percentage of fuel used for industrial steam and hot water which can be covered by CHP, by sector, the Netherlands

Sector	Potential coverage by CHP (%)
Paper, pulp and printing	91
Food and drink	61
Non-ferrous metals	20
Chemical and petrochemical	19

The Netherlands

The 1987 CHP Stimulation Programme has the following characteristics:

- there are subsidies available, which reduce the payback period, making CHP more commercially viable;
- covenants made between government and industry stimulate target setting and the preparation of environmental action plans;
- utilities invest directly in CHP, or form joint ventures with an industrial company;
- targets set by utilities include: energy distribution companies to achieve 4000 MW_e of CHP installed by the year 2000; electricity production companies to achieve 1000 MW_e; District Heating CHP of 1000 MW_e to be installed.

As a result, from 1990 to 1993, 270 MW_e were installed per annum.

Denmark

Under the provisions of the Heat Supply Act revised (1990):

- new electricity capacity must be based on small-scale CHP plants fuelled by natural gas, refuse or biomass;
- municipalities must ensure that access to local heat markets is available to potential CHP operators. Municipalities have the right to impose compulsory connection of consumers to the district heating network.

Financial incentives include:

- favourable buy-back tariffs (based on avoided costs of coal-fired plant with SO_x and NO_x abatement and avoided distribution costs);
- grid connection costs paid for by independent power producers;
- a percentage of natural gas is priced for CHP users at half the price paid by heating-only boilers;
- new electricity capacity must be based on small-scale CHP plants fuelled by natural gas, refuse or biomass;
- municipalities must ensure that access to local heat markets is available to potential CHP operators. Municipalities have the right to impose compulsory connection of consumers to the district heating network.

In 1990, as a result of these measures, almost 50 per cent of non-industrial heating market was provided through district heating.

Regulation

In the 1970s, in the Netherlands it was not permitted to use more than 10 million M^3 (later increased to 30 million M^3) of natural gas per annum in steam boilers, that is, not in CHP or combined-cycle gas turbines. This policy was introduced in order to conserve Dutch gas supplies; it was abolished in 1983.

It has been estimated that if the restriction of 30 million m^3 were still applied, about 1600 MW_e of CHP would have to be installed, spread over 23 plants, equivalent to 9 per cent of Dutch power capacity and achieving a reduction of 4.7 million tonnes of CO_2.

Pricing

Table 6.14   Buy-back tariffs for electricity (ECU per kWh)

Country	Biomass	CHP
Belgium	3.3	3.3
Denmark	7.9	4.7
France	3.7	3.3
Germany	7.0	4.7
Italy	13.0	6.5
Netherlands	3.7	3.7
UK	7.4	2.8

Price terms for buy-back and wheeling (selling excess electricity directly to another user via the public grid) are significant influences on the attractiveness of CHP. Wheeling is not allowed in Denmark, Greece, Spain, or Luxembourg and rarely in Germany. The buy-back price for CHP-produced electricity is compared with that provided by biomass produced electricity in Table 6.14.

Conclusions on Regulation and Combined Heat and Power (CHP)

- Only two European countries – Denmark and the Netherlands – have made serious efforts over the past decade to encourage combined heat and power (CHP).
- They have succeeded in increasing the share of CHP in power generation and energy use by a combination of grants, relatively favourable buy-back arrangements, favourable prices for natural gas, regulations on the use of waste heat and licensing of power producers.
- A regulation limiting the annual use of natural gas in steam boilers (now abolished) would result in an investment in CHP capacity installed

---

Box 6.3
Lessons for policy makers on the stimulation of combined heat and power (CHP) to achieve energy conservation

1. *If it is desired to increase the share of energy production using CHP, a combination of subsidies, regulations (such as that requiring municipalities to ensure that access to local heat markets is available to local CHP operators) and non-discrimination against CHP-produced electricity via wheeling and buy-back will achieve the objective.*
   CHP in the Netherlands and Denmark has grown rapidly in recent years in response to such a policy mix.

2. *A Dutch regulation limiting access to natural gas for steam boilers (that is, boilers not using CHP or combined-cycle gas turbines) would, if it still applied, result in about 1600 MW$_e$ of CHP installed, equivalent to 9 per cent of the country's power capacity.*
   This policy was only applied in the Netherlands for a short while, so the implications are of necessity somewhat speculative.

3. *But there are no estimates available of the total costs and benefits of such combinations.*

Note: This information is based on the detailed analysis in Chapter 3.

---

amounting to 9 per cent of total Dutch power capacity, and a reduction of 4.7 million tonnes of CO_2.

- CHP has been discriminated against in most countries in terms of the price which 'surplus' electricity commands compared with renewables.

DEMAND-SIDE MANAGEMENT (DSM)

Demand-side measures are taken by an electricity supplier or other party (apart from the electricity consumer) to reduce a consumer's demand for electricity through improvements in the efficiency with which it is used. Demand-side measures can range from provision of information to direct investment by the utility in improving customers' energy efficiency. The main policy objective of DSM is to ensure that increments in energy conservation are not discriminated against *vis-à-vis* increments in energy supply.

Integrated resource planning (IRP) in the USA requires utilities to assess all resource options to meet customers' needs, including the promotion of efficient end-use devices; all the costs and benefits to society should be considered in making choices.

Policies to stimulate DSM may be some combination of: regulation (mandated); integrated resource plans; comparison of demand-side and supply-side options (information); financial incentives (making DSM profitable); accounting for environmental externalities. In Europe levies to raise finance for DSM, utility targets for CO_2 emissions and decoupling revenues from sales are amongst the specific measures used. In the UK, privatization of electricity production and distribution has produced a number of regional electricity companies (production) and a national distribution company, the National Grid Company. An independent regulator determines the price which producers and the distribution company can charge. The regulator has taken some decisions which should be favourable to DSM, including decoupling the price from the units sold, on the basis that most of the costs at the margin of production, sale and distribution are only partially related to volume of electricity (see Table 6.15).

The UK government set up an Energy Saving Trust as its vehicle to achieve 25 per cent of the UK's CO_2 reduction target, to be financed via a levy on consumers' gas and electricity bills. The regulators have refused to sanction such a move.

Table 6.15   Weighting factors in UK electricity pricing formula (% of total)

	Customers (%)	kWh sold (%)	Total
Supply	75	25	100
Distribution	50	50	100

COSTS AND BENEFITS OF DSM (DOMESTIC LIGHTING)

The costs include the utilities' investments necessary to purchase, market, deliver and install energy efficiency measures. The benefits include the electricity generation, transmission and distribution costs that are avoided.

Is the cost of conserved energy (CCE) less than the avoided costs? In a study of experience in ten European countries between 1987 and 1991, which was designed to increase the use of energy-efficient compact fluorescent lights (CFLs), the average societal cost was estimated at mECU22 per kWh, which was only one-third the cost of building and operating new electric power plants. The following lessons were yielded:

- the programme was most effective where a high proportion of the cost of efficient lamps was subsidized (strong interest was shown by consumers at a price of ECU7–10 per lamp);
- information-only strategies achieve very low penetration rates;
- the form of incentive (pay on bills) is as important as the magnitude of incentive;
- non-economic factors very important;
- women respond differently from men;
- pensioners and occupants of single-family homes are over-represented in relation to their share of the total population.

The Holyhead (Wales) Experience with Encouraging Compact Fluorescent Lighting (CFL)

Holyhead was served by two regional transformers which were in danger of becoming overloaded. 'Normal' growth (2 per cent per annum) would require an investment of £750 000 in the distribution network within two years: the financial logic of the programme flowed from the desirability of postponing this investment. This would be achieved if peak electricity demand could be reduced from 9 MW to 8 MW within six months. A package was provided offering two energy-efficient light bulbs at the same price as conventional bulbs, free lagging of immersion hot-water cylinders, and discounted loft insulation and draught-proofing. In the case of the lighting programme, the hall, landing and lounge were targeted. Notwithstanding very active promotion, 22 per cent of households did not participate.

The figures in Table 6.16 imply that the programme had a net cost. However, the benefit estimate does not evaluate the benefits accruing as a result of deferring the £750 000 investment in distribution, which was a primary motivation for the project. If this was deferred by, say, six years, and the real interest rate is 7 per cent, then the saving is:

$$£750\ 000 - £750\ 000/(1.07)^6 = £750\ 000 - £750\ 000/1.501$$
$$= £750\ 000 - £449\ 667 = £300\ 333$$

Such a gain would yield a net benefit. The avoided cost per kilovolt-ampere (kVA) saved was £291, which is considerably lower than the avoided cost of new combined-cycle gas turbines.

Table 6.16   The estimated costs and benefits of the demand-side management programme, Holyhead, Wales

	Net present value (ECU000)
Programme costs	162
Avoided costs (programme benefits)	101
Balance	–61

The Energy Saving Trust Pilot Scheme

In the UK, the Trust launched a scheme to promote the sale of CFL in conjunction with lighting manufacturers, with the support of most of the regional electricity companies. The results were very encouraging, yielding a substantial net benefit. However, the energy saving benefits estimate needs to be treated with caution: it is not based on a post-programme analysis, but is a 'best estimate' only (Table 6.17).

Table 6.17   Compact fluorescent lamp (CFL) promotion by Energy Savings Trust, UK

	Net present value (ECU000)
Programme costs	8 612
Avoided costs (benefits)	14 892
Balance	6 280

The results show that under certain conditions there are net benefits to be captured with DSM programmes, even without quantifying the environmental gain; that there are benefits from economies of scale – all-country coverage – as compared with the results in Holyhead, where the client group was very small; that there is a need to design the policy framework such that utilities have incentives to act on the opportunities implicit in DSM.

Box 6.4

Lessons for policy-makers on the use of demand-side management (DSM) to achieve energy conservation

1. *Under certain conditions, DSM can yield substantial net benefits.*

2. *Crucial in this regard is the achievement of economies of scale; there are considerable start-up and administrative costs.*

3. *Providing the right incentives to utilities is crucial. In practice, pricing policy must be designed (for example, uncoupling revenue from units sold) such that net revenues do not suffer as a consequence of embracing DSM.*

4. *In the case of compact fluorescent lighting (CFL), a combination of subsidy (pay on bills) and information is required to achieve significant take-up.*

5. *Marketing skills and technique are central elements.*

Note: This information is based on the detailed analysis in Chapter 4.

INSTITUTIONAL DESIGN: AREA IMPLEMENTATION OF ENERGY CONSERVATION IN FRANCE

The initial institutional response in France after the first oil 'shock' in 1973 was highly centralized (the Agency for Energy Savings: AEE), undertaking the formulation of national regulations, organizing energy efficiency inspections (mandatory after 1977 for thermal installations which consume more than 300 tonnes of oil equivalent: TOE) and evaluating investment proposals for subsidy. The regulations made insulation of buildings mandatory and created a market for efficient space-heating systems; the latter favoured low capital cost electric heating. The subsidy programme provided a capital grant of FFr400 for an annual TOE estimated energy saved.

In 1982, coincident with the introduction of regionalization in French government, the French Agency for Energy Management (AFME) was formed, which combined AEE with other agencies, broadened its brief to include renewable energies and research, and decentralized its functions. In particular, it used the Special Fund for Large Operations (FSGT – financed by an additional tax on motor fuels) from 1982 to 1987 in conjunction with the Regional Funds for Energy Management (FRMEs). To administer this programme, regional branches were established in conjunction with the regional governments; each application was judged on its merits, with priority given to conservation investments which, without support, would not be financially viable.

The latest institutional development is the creation of ADEME (Agency for Environment and Energy Management), which broadens the scope further to include air and noise pollution. But in recent years (since 1986) budgets for energy conservation have been very significantly reduced.

Energy conservation and diversification performance in France mirror experience elsewhere, with very large reductions in energy consumption by industry, stabilization by households, but with a shift in the mix away from coal and oil and towards natural gas and electricity, and substantial increases in transport (2 per cent per annum between 1973 and 1990).

Between 1974 and 1981, a simple subsidy was available which provided a grant of FFr400 per TOE saved, to support investment in conservation where it could be demonstrated that this would save 1 TOE. From 1982 to 1992, a grant was provided based on the specifics of a proposal submitted, but designed to maximize conservation performance (see Table 6.18).

Table 6.18   Subsidies for energy conservation, France, 1974–93

Sector	Subsidy (ECU billion)	Total investment (ECU billion)
Industry	0.55	2.10
Domestic and service	0.43	1.65

The performance of these investments (and those in transport) were estimated for 20 000 representative projects which were implemented, using the actual energy prices which prevailed over the study period. The benefit is the value of the energy savings achieved by consumers; the cost is the total investment (including subsidy) and operating costs. The difference between gross value of savings and the costs of achieving same are estimated in Table 6.19.

Table 6.20 shows the distribution of the energy conservation investment over time. The estimates are based on *ex ante* (before implementation) calculations. However, some *ex post* evaluations were carried out which indicated that the projected savings were in fact achieved, at least in the large operations. It is not appropriate to 'attribute' all of this gain to the subsidies, for two reasons: there were other policy instruments operating (information via subsidy of audits, regulations concerning building insulation, research support) which happened in parallel with the subsidy programme; second, no effort is made to separate the investments which would have happened anyway (the free-riders). However, after 1982, only investments which would not have been financially viable were supported, so this proportion of the portfolio should not suffer from the free-rider problem.

Table 6.19   Net savings resulting from conservation investment, France, 1975–2007 (Millions of Constant 1992 ECUs)

Year	Net savings
1975	−39
1977	−1040
1979	−1780
1981	−199
1983	2187
1985	3510
1987	4173
1991	6528
1995	8033
1999	8691
2003	8904
2007	8929

Table 6.20   Investment in conservation in France, 1975–92 (1992 ECU)

Period	Number	Subsidies (mill. ECU)	Total invest. (mill. ECU)	Avg. invest. (ECU)	Avg. subsidy (ECU)	Total NPV (mill. ECU)
1975–82	3 873	282	2097	540 000	72 000	14 503
1983–86	25 000	574	2359	100 000	23 000	449
1987–92	3 435	84	592	170 000	24 000	−152
Total	32 308	940	5048			14 800

There is a pattern of reducing financial returns to the conservation investment, for two reasons: the first package (ECU400 grant per TOE saved) was taken up mainly by the large industrial firms which could achieve immediate benefits, and in some cases would have taken up the investment without the grant; second, diminishing returns to investment are likely to set in over time, as the most financially attractive investments are taken up first. For the investments in the 1987–92 period to make sense nationally, *external benefits* – benefits not captured directly by those making the investment – need to be generated.

External Benefits

There is also a substantial reduction achieved in CO_2 – 3 per cent of the level of emissions in 1992 – but little reduction in nitrogen oxide emissions, because these are mainly from the transportation sector where progress was least successful in achieving conservation. The programme also reduced energy imports and therefore had a positive impact on the balance of payments, and also (by reducing demand) on the equilibrium price of energy.

Institutional and Operational Implications

- Over the 1975–82 period, a highly centralized programme with a very simple test (ECU400 grant per TOE saved with no other restrictions) produced large energy and financial gains, although some of these would have happened without the subsidy. This policy type favoured a relatively small number of large industrial enterprises (see Table 6.20) which had the technical and financial means to benefit quickly from conservation investment. But there was very little innovation and very little dissemination of technologies and know-how.
- The Regional Funds for Energy Management (FRMEs) operating over the 1983–6 period favoured linkage, innovation, local action and partnership, and were very successful in encouraging innovation, generating local action and, in particular, in supporting small and medium-sized enterprises (SMEs). They only supported projects where the 'private' returns alone would not be sufficient to justify the investment, so that they in effect 'screened out' of public support those projects which on paper would have shown the highest returns.
- For the period 1987–92, public funding was reduced, and projects were largely confined to small-scale projects with a significant innovation element, where demonstration effects were likely.

There are some lessons to be learnt from French experience with regional teams. A successful team will have:

- a capacity to contract with territorial authorities: setting joint objectives and programmes, project design, the designation of partners for dissemination;
- effective use of existing public and private transmission networks: such networks include (but are not confined to) chambers of commerce, consumer associations, local authorities, domestic appliance equipment suppliers and technical associations;
- effective communication of choices to networks and to the network partners: targeted communication is much more effective than national-level exhortation or image building;
- appropriate tools, including:

  — standard methods of information generation and evaluation; for example, the adoption of the thermal audit method invented in 1980 which was used by all in the evaluation of proposed energy conservation investments in existing buildings;

— links to national agencies and to the most up-to-date demonstration and research results;

— the capacity and willingness to compare and to evaluate on technical, economic, institutional and social grounds;

- the ability to mobilize finance from a variety of sources: such as grant, third-party financing, charges, partnerships with banks, and link its provision to performance;
- policy evaluation, to identify causes of success and failure, and provide a basis for modification thereof.

Box 6.5

Lessons for Policy-makers on institutional design to achieve energy conservation

1. *To achieve large energy savings quickly, concentrate on the largest industrial combines; don't worry about 'free-rider' problems; and put in place a very simple and generous incentive package.*
   The French 400 ECU grant per TOE saved was of this character.

2. *A highly centralized national organization is best suited to 'capture' this market for energy conservation.*

3. *If the free-riders (those who would have undertaken the investment anyway) can be identified and not grant aided, this will reduce the conservation performance as judged (inappropriately) on a crude basis of conservation achieved relative to grant paid.*

4. *Regionalization is necessary to achieve education, training, a focus on SMEs and confining the support to those who would not undertake the investment in its absence.*

5. *For regional teams to be successful, they must have: the capacity to contract with other regional and national authorities; the ability to make effective use of existing public and private transmission networks; the ability to mobilize finance from a variety of sources; a critical mass in terms of scope and scale – a region of 2 million people would need a unit with a staff of 15–20 and an annual budget of over ECU4 million.*

Note: This information is based on the detailed analysis in Chapter 5.

Team Character and Size

A 'typical' team for a region of 2 million population would comprise 15–20 people and cost a total (salaries, premises, operating costs) of ECU1.5 million annually. Such a team could supervise (from inception, evaluation and investment) 200 projects annually.

An annual volume of subsidy in the range of ECU2.5–5 million supervised by such a team should have associated with it a total investment of ECU20–30 million Table 6.21. In addition, in the French case, much of the teams' work would involve the provision of information and undertaking of technical studies, training, development and nurturing of networks, performance evaluation and help in locating finance.

Table 6.21   Costs and implications of a typical regional energy conservation team, France

Annual costs (ECU000)		
Operating		1 500
Grant aid to industry		1 200
Grant aid to households, commerce, agriculture, renewables		1 200
Extension services (network development, training, etc.)		380
Total		4 280
Energy savings over investment lifetime	TOE 000	ECU000
Industry	10 000	15 000
Households, commerce, agriculture, renewables	1 120	7 300
Extension services	3 133	7 400
Total	14 253	29 700
Reduction in environmental impacts		
per annum (000 tonnes)		
CO_2	1,900	
SO_2	36	
NO_x	3	

REFERENCES

Commission of the European Communities (CEC) (1994), *Achievements and Results of the ExternE Project*, Brussels: The Commission.

CEPN, ETSU, Ecole des Mines, IER and Metroeconomica (1994), *Externalities of Fuel Cycles: ExternE Project, Summary Report*, Brussels: European Commission, DG XII.

Index

ACE, 81
action pointers, 4
actors, 127–8, 135–6
  organization of on-site actors, 132–4
ADEME (Agency for the Environment
  and Energy Management), 111,
  113, 160
administrative homogeneity, 109, 137–8
administrative logic, 139
advice: written, 40–44, 150–51
advice centres, 38–40, 46
AFME (French Agency for Energy
  Management), 110–11, 112, 115,
  124, 128, 159
Agency for Energy Savings (AEE), 106,
  110, 111, 115, 159
alternatives: comparison of, 135
ANRED (National Agency for Waste
  Recuperation), 111
AQA (Air Quality Agency), 111
'as the world turns' logic, 139
attic insulation grant scheme, 7–8
audits
  Denmark, 44–5
  France, 109–10
  Germany, 38–44, 150–51
Austria, 84
autoproducers: and CHP, 49–51, 53
  see also energy companies
avoided costs, 79–80
  lighting programmes, 91–3, 96, 97
  UK electricity, 79–80, 100–101
avoided emissions, 63–4, 123

Belgium, 51–2, 54
Bergman, H., 5
'Best Practice' information programme,
  20
Blok, K., 56, 57, 58, 59, 61, 63
Boardman, B., 10, 15, 16

boilers, 22, 42
  natural gas and steam boilers, 61, 62
  registration scheme, 45
Brabazon, P., 11
Brand, M., 59
Bretagne, 122
budgetary procedures, 6–7, 13
Brown, M., 54
Building Research Energy Conservation
  Support Unit (BRECSU) 18
Bund-Länder-Programm, 24
Busch, J.F., 61
business sector: subsidies to, 19–20
buy-back tariffs, 64–8, 154–5

California Public Utility Commission
  (PUC), 73
capacity to contract, 135–6
capping, 101
carbon dioxide emissions, 2
  regulation, 63–4
  targets, 75, 95
CEC, 2, 144
cellar ceiling insulation, 43
central heating boilers *see* boilers
CEPN, 30, 32, 145
chimney-sweeps, 40–44, 46, 150–51
Christensen, I.M., 45
Clausnitzer, K.-D., 37
Cline, W.R., 33
coal prices: future, 2
combined heat and power (CHP), 48–70,
  152–6
  development of capacity, 49–54
  economic instruments, 64–8, 154–5
  policy recommendations, 68–9
  potentials for in the EU, 54–7
  regulation *see* regulation
communication policies, 136

165

Energy Action Grant Agency (EAGA), 15, 16, 146–7
Energy Action programme, 8–10, 28
energy buses, 38, 39
energy companies, 58–9, 61, 68–9
see also autoproducers
Energy Management Assistance Scheme, 19–20
Energy Saving Trust (EST), 77, 156
promotion of CFLs, 94–9, 158
energy savings: influence of regulation on, 63–4
Energy 2000 programme, 54
Enfield Green House project, 17, 18
environmental benefits, 94, 98–9
environmental externalities, 74
environmental licences, 63
environmental protection, 46
EPRI, 81
European Union (EU), 4, 81, 137
CHP, 48–70, 152–6
development of CHP capacity, 49–54
economic instruments, 64–8
policy recommendations, 68–9
potentials for CHP, 54–7
regulation, 58–64
DSM, 74–5, 156
cost/benefit analysis of lighting programmes, 84–99
lighting programmes, 82–4, 157–8
exchange rates, 29
expenses: reduction of, 116–18
expertise, 137
external benefits, 80
valuing, 144–5, 161–2
external costs, 2, 30–33, 144
ExternE project, 2, 32

Fankhauser, S., 30, 33
Farla, J., 58
Federal Ministry of Economics, 37, 38–40
financial incentives
CHP, 64–8, 154–5
DSM, 74
financial partnerships, 138–9
financial resources: nature of, 138
financing, 137–8
foreign exchange, 123

400 francs per TOE procedure, 111, 132, 160, 161, 162
comparative analysis, 124–31
4.35 Billion DM Programm, 24
France, 105–42, 159–64
CHP, 51–2, 54
energy management policies, 108–12
institutional policies, 110–11
regulation, 108–10
energy policy context, 106–8
lighting programmes, 84–5
regional teams *see* regional teams
subsidies *see* subsidies
free-drivers, 80, 91, 97
free-riders, 79, 91, 97, 120, 130
French Agency for Energy Management (AFME), 110–11, 112, 115, 124, 128, 159
FRMEs (Regional Funds for Energy Management), 111, 112, 115, 134, 159, 162
comparative analysis, 124–31
FSGT (Special Fund for Large Operations), 111–12, 120, 133, 159
comparative analysis, 124–31

Gärtner, M., 33
Germany, 3
CHP, 51–2
consultation programmes, 37–47, 150–51
advice centres and audits, 38–40
Hessen pilot programmes, 40–44
grants and subsidies, 23–4, 148–9
lighting programmes, 85
GIS, 38
global warming: damage estimates, 30–33, 144–5
government investment *see* direct investment
graduated rent subsidies, 23
grants and subsidies, 6–36, 143, 145–9
Denmark, 24–5, 27
Germany, 23–4, 148–9
Ireland, 6–14, 25–6, 27, 28, 145–6, 149
Netherlands, 21–3, 26–7, 148
policy recommendations, 28–9
UK, 14–21, 26–7, 146–8, 149
grassroots organizations, 4